Beyond Instinct: The Philosophy of Autognosis

Copyright Page

Beyond Instinct: The Philosophy of Autognosis
Copyright © 2025 by Robert Horodyski
All rights reserved.

No part of this book may be reproduced, stored in a retrieval system, or transmitted in any form or by any means—electronic, mechanical, photocopying, recording, or otherwise—without prior written permission of the publisher, except in the case of brief quotations embodied in critical articles and reviews.

Cover and interior design by the author. Published by Harbinger Holdings LLC

ISBN: 979-8-9988889-7-7
First Edition, 2025

Printed in the United States of America

Dedication

For those who have ever felt lost in their own agency, helpless to shape their world. If you have sensed the quiet pull of instincts steering your choices, yet longed to chart a different course. For the ones *willing* to rise, reflect, and author the story of their own becoming – this book is for you.

Acknowledgments

No philosophy is created in isolation. Though the framework of Autognosis is my own, it stands upon the work, insights, and courage of many others. I am indebted to the thinkers whose explorations of cognition, instinct, and freedom laid the ground on which these ideas could grow—Kahneman, Beck, Hayes, Sapolsky, and the long lineage of philosophers and teachers who sought to help humanity see itself clearly.

I am grateful to those who engaged with early drafts of these ideas, who questioned, challenged, and strengthened the philosophy by refusing easy answers. To friends, colleagues, and readers who carried conversations further than I could alone: thank you.

Finally, to those whose struggles with instinct—fear, anger, shame, belonging—reminded me that this work is not abstract, but urgent and human. This book is dedicated to you, and to the possibility for humanity to live beyond instinct.

Note on Terminology

Some common terms that may be unfamiliar or used in slightly different ways than in other contexts. To avoid confusion:

- **Autognosis**: aw-tohg-NOH-siss- From the Greek *auto* (self) and *gnosis* (knowledge). Here it refers to literacy of instinctual signals and the practice of conscious self-authorship.

- **Autopilot:** The default state of living by instinct without awareness or authorship.

- **Freedom:** In this book, freedom refers to individual free will — not political or social freedom.

- **Obsolescent Instincts:** Primal signals no longer aligned with modern society.

- **Redirection**: The practice of channeling impulse energy into aligned, constructive action rather than suppressing or indulging it.

- **Reflection and Design**: The cycle of reviewing behavior patterns and intentionally encoding principles, rituals, and structures into one's life.

- **Signal/Drive/Impulse**: Any instinctual drive or biological impulse (fear, dominance, belonging, etc.) rooted in evolutionary programming. These terms are used interchangeably throughout.

- **Signal/Instinct Literacy**: The ability to recognize, name, and track these impulses with precision.

Preface

Much of what we call human choice is not choice at all. Beneath the language of freedom and reason, most behavior is driven by ancient impulses—fear, dominance, belonging, hunger, and status—that evolved for survival in a world long gone. These signals, once useful, now misfire in modern conditions, distorting decisions at every scale, from personal relationships to global governance.

The philosophy of **Autognosis** emerged as a response to this recognition. The term means "self-knowledge," but not in the traditional sense of identity or narrative. Instead, Autognosis is the literacy of instincts—the ability to read, separate from, and redirect biological signals rather than obey them blindly. It is the practice of authorship: constructing an intentional self, rather than being run by default code written millions of years ago.

This book, *Beyond Instinct: The Philosophy of Autognosis,* is not a technical manual, nor is it an abstract philosophical treatise. It is a bridge between science, philosophy, and lived experience. It lays bare the biological roots of human dysfunction, presents a method for conscious override, and imagines what a society built on self-authorship might look like. The aim is ambitious but urgent: to equip individuals—and by extension, civilizations—with the tools to move beyond instinct and into design.

The chapters that follow are organized in three parts:

- **Part I** examines the biological substrate and the problem of autopilot.

- **Part II** introduces Autognosis as philosophy and practice.
- **Part III** is the nuts and bolts of Autognosis. It provides tools, protocols, and framework for applying the concepts.
- **Part IV** is the vision for the future lived through instinct literacy.

Along the way, readers will encounter signal maps, redirection toolkits, and design protocols—practical methods for transforming awareness into agency.

This book is written as both diagnosis and invitation. The diagnosis: our civilization is built on unchecked biology, and without intervention, it will consume itself in the same way past civilization have done. The invitation: each individual has the power to reclaim authorship of their mind and life, and in doing so, contribute to a new stage of human evolution.

Whether you are a student of philosophy, a seeker of self-mastery, or simply someone who feels the weight of a world driven by reaction, my hope is that these pages offer both clarity and direction. Autognosis is not mine alone; it belongs to anyone willing to practice it. What follows is not just a philosophy, but a blueprint for freedom—one that begins not with the world, but with you.

Table of Contents

Front Matter
- Copyright Page
- Dedication
- Acknowledgments
- Note on Terminology
- Preface

Part I – The Problem

Chapter 1: A World on Autopilot............... 1
- Personal Prologue
- The Autopilot Condition
- The Mismatch Problem
- Examples in Daily Life
- A Solution- Autognosis

Chapter 2: The Hidden Code of Instinct........... 13
- The Concept of Code
- The Core Drives
- The Autopilot in Action
- The Layer of Illusion
- Necessity of Intervention

Chapter 3: Civilization as an Extension of the Individual.................................. 25
- Civilization Instinct
- Historical Patterns
- Modern Case Studies
- The Substrate Problem
- Recursive Dysfunction
- Society Re-imagined

Part II – The Philosophy

Chapter 4: Autognosis Defined...................... 37
- The Name and its Meaning
- The Five Pillars Explained
- How it Differs From Other Traditions
- Autognosis as an Operating System
- A Universal but Flexible Model

Chapter 5: Freedom is Built, Not Given........... 51
- The Illusion of Default Freedom
- Freedom as a Discipline
- Historical and Philosophical Roots
- Training Autonomy
- Everyday Proof of Concept

Chapter 6: The Engineering of Selfhood.......... 63
- The Myth of Fixed Self
- The Self as a System
- Engineering the Self
- Examples in Practice
- The Promise of Systemic Selfhood

Part III – The Practice

Chapter 7: Recognition- Signal Literacy.......... 79
- What is Signal Literacy
- The Core Maps of Signals
- Everyday Examples
- Tools for Building Fluency
- The Challenge of Overlap
- From Knowledge to Action

Chapter 8: Separation- You Are Not Your Impulse... 99
- Importance of Separation
- Scientific Basis
- Practices of Separation
- Drills and Tools
- Developmental Scaling
- Outcome

Chapter 9: The Redirection Toolkit................ 105
- Why Redirection Matters
- The Principles of Redirection
- Redirection Models
- Practical Toolkit
- Case Studies and Vignettes
- Common Pitfalls
- True Redirection has Three Markers

Chapter 10: Reflection and Design.................. 119
- The Power of Reflection
- Reflection Tools
- The Transition to Design
- Design Components
- Practical Exercises
- Engineering Authorship

Part IV – The Horizon

Chapter 11: Autognosis in Society.................. 131
- Systems Mirror Biology
- Education and Early Intervention
- Leadership and Governance
- Justice and Conflict Resolution
- Economics and Resource Management

- Media and Culture
- Institutional Case Studies
- Objections and Challenges
- In Summary

Chapter 12: Autognosis and the Future............ 149
- The Next Evolutionary Leap
- Technology and AI
- Post-Instinctual Civilization
- Environmental Imperatives
- The Risk of Regression
- Speculative Horizons
- Ethics of the Future

Chapter 13: Invitation to the Reader............... 163
- The Threshold Question
- The Mirror Moment
- Personal Agency
- The Scale of Impact
- The Invitation
- Closing Vision

Afterword.. 171

Part I – The Problem

Chapter 1. A World on Autopilot

Personal Prologue:

I remember the moment when the scale of it all hit me. The weight of humanity's cage—not made of iron bars, but of centuries of habit, institutions, reflexes, and instincts. It felt immovable, a monolith of biology and culture that pressed down on every attempt at change. But then a second recognition followed, equally sobering and strangely liberating: this cage is not an object. It's people. Just people.

Individuals who eat, sleep, doubt, fear, and sometimes—if only rarely—change.

The immensity of systems—governments, economies, religions, empires—can fool us into imagining them as external powers, as though they were gods directing our lives. But they are emergent, not immutable. Strip them down and you find the same fragile creatures underneath: humans with impulses, neuroses, and blind spots no different from our own. Recognizing this collapses the mystique.

Still, the paradox persists. On one hand, the scale of the system is crushing. On the other, the levers are always at the individual level. One person cannot topple the whole, but one person can alter the trajectory of another. And that ripple, multiplied, is how cultures bend across time.

This realization was both heavy and clarifying. Heavy, because it meant there is no shortcut—no deus ex machina waiting to save us. Clarifying, because it meant the power to redirect civilization's arc lies within the smallest unit: the individual. Autognosis was born from that recognition. This book focuses on the biological roots of humanity's dysfunction, with the hope that addressing them will inherently influence the cultural conditions.

The Autopilot Condition:

Human beings like to imagine themselves as rational actors, steering their lives with intention and foresight. Yet much of daily behavior runs on a kind of evolutionary autopilot. The same instinctual signals that once kept our ancestors alive on the savannah now fire relentlessly in environments for which they were never designed and have not evolved to match. For the majority of human existence these instincts were in line with our survival. However, in the last few millennia, a micro-second in evolutionary terms, the industrialization and modernization of society has significantly changed the landscape of life. We have gone from small tribes of hunter-gatherers, driven primarily by sex, hunger, and aggression, to a hyperconnected, industrial, digital civilization where those same drives dictate our actions. The result is a chronic misalignment of impulses once optimized for survival that no longer fit modern life

Consider the **fear signal**. Fear evolved as a rapid threat-detection system—an invaluable reflex when predators lurked in the tall grass. In modern life, this signal still triggers instantly, but without lions or wolves, it attaches to abstract or exaggerated threats: stock market fluctuations, political rivals, online criticism. Instead of mobilizing energy to flee or fight, fear now drives cycles of anxiety, polarization, and chronic stress.

Or take **status competition**. Among early humans, reputation and dominance determined access to mates, food, and protection. Today, the same drive plays out in social media "likes," corporate hierarchies, and consumerism. Billboards and influencer feeds hijack this circuitry, teaching us to equate manufactured symbols—cars, clothing, follower counts—with survival itself. The instinct that once kept a tribe's hierarchy functional now fuels debt, envy, and compulsive overconsumption.

The **tribal belonging drive** is another case. Evolution wired us to align with in-groups because exclusion meant death. In modern pluralistic societies, this impulse often manifests as political partisanship, nationalism, or online echo chambers. Belonging is still treated as existential, but now it fractures humanity into countless hostile subgroups—each clinging to identity markers as if their lives depended on it.

Even **scarcity behaviors**, once vital for storing calories through lean seasons, now misfire in abundance. The instinct to hoard drives overfilled pantries, compulsive shopping, and wasteful accumulation. On a global scale, this has led to environmental depletion—forests clear-cut, oceans overfished, carbon burned—because the impulse to "take while it's available" still overrides rational long-term planning.

These examples reveal a consistent pattern: ancient circuits firing in novel conditions, producing maladaptive results. The autopilot condition is not malicious—it is simply obsolete. Yet unless recognized and redirected, it governs the majority of human life, from how individuals eat and argue to how civilizations wage war and collapse.

The Mismatch Problem:

Evolution is not a process that optimizes for truth, fairness, or flourishing. It optimizes for reproductive success within a specific environment. Human instincts were calibrated in conditions of scarcity, small-group living, and immediate survival pressures. When those conditions shift—as they have radically in the last few millennia—the instincts do not update at the same pace. This lag is the essence of the **mismatch problem**: behaviors that were once adaptive now become destructive.

Anthropologists estimate that over **95% of human evolutionary history** occurred in hunter-gatherer contexts. Meaning our cognitive architecture reflects that legacy. A tribe of 150 individuals, a limited territory, and seasonal rhythms of food availability shaped the drives for status, fear, belonging, and control. Yet in the span of only a few hundred generations, humans moved into cities of millions, created agricultural and industrial surpluses, and built digital networks linking billions. The environment transformed, but the signal set remained essentially the same.

This mismatch manifests everywhere, here are just a few examples:

- **Caloric preference**: Sweetness and fat were rare and precious to early humans, triggering strong reward pathways. Today, they are mass-produced and ubiquitous, driving obesity and metabolic disease.

- **Aggression**: Quick retaliation once deterred threats in face-to-face tribal conflicts. In modern geopolitics, the same impulse escalates disputes between nuclear powers.

- **Reciprocity bias**: Favoring those who give immediate rewards worked in small tribes. In complex economies, it leaves individuals vulnerable to manipulation by advertisers, populist leaders, and scam artists.

- **Present bias**: Focusing on immediate gains rather than long-term consequences was advantageous in uncertain environments. In global civilization, it produces short-sighted policy, debt culture, and environmental collapse.

The critical point is not that instincts are "bad." They are simply **out of context**. What kept humans alive in the Pleistocene now undermines stability in the

Anthropocene. Civilization rests on mismatched foundations: outdated biological algorithms running inside modern technological frameworks.

Unless this mismatch is recognized and consciously corrected, it guarantees recurring cycles of dysfunction. Reforms and revolutions repeatedly fail because they address the surface—laws, structures, ideologies—without rewriting the substrate. Beneath the slogans and manifestos, the same limbic code continues to drive behavior.

Autognosis begins by confronting this mismatch directly. It does not blame individuals for their biology, but it refuses to let biology alone determine destiny. The next step is to examine, in detail, how these mismatches play out in the institutions that shape collective life.

Examples in Daily Life:

The mismatch between instinct and environment is not confined to history books or global crises. It is present in the routines of daily life, shaping choices so seamlessly that most people never notice the underlying signals.

At the office. A colleague is promoted, and envy rises before you can even think. The signal has nothing to do with survival—it's a status threat reflex from a time when rank meant food and protection. Yet it influences how you speak to them, whether you collaborate, even how you interpret their success. An ancient drive spills into a modern workplace, breeding resentment and competition where cooperation would serve everyone better.

At the store. A discount sign flashes "limited time only." Scarcity bias, once vital for seizing resources before they vanished, now triggers an impulse purchase of something unnecessary. The instinct does not ask whether the item is useful, only whether it might be lost. Retailers have perfected the art of pressing this button, turning a survival algorithm into a business model.

On social media. A photo receives fewer likes than expected. Belonging circuitry, honed for tight-knit tribes, interprets this as a threat of exclusion. Anxiety builds—not because the digital reaction has any real survival stakes, but because the brain cannot distinguish between physical ostracism and virtual indifference. The signal was once about staying alive in a group; now it erodes self-worth with every scroll.

In conversation. A disagreement escalates quickly, voices rising, a surge of adrenaline. Anger was designed to establish boundaries and deter threats in direct encounters. But in modern life, this surge often derails relationships, replacing reason with defensiveness. What was once a tool of survival becomes a wedge between friends, partners, or colleagues.

In social rituals. The drive for belonging—once a safeguard against exile and death—now expresses itself in rituals like drinking culture. Alcohol is not magical in itself; it functions as a shortcut, muting the signals of exclusion and insecurity. By raising the same glass, sharing the same toast, and lowering the same inhibitions, people mimic connection without confronting those instincts directly. The signal does not account for authenticity; it only shouts "belong." Millions join shallow rituals that feel sincere in the moment but collapse on reflection, not because they lack real desire for connection, but because the autopilot signal is firing in the wrong environment.

Each of these examples shares the same source: a signal optimized for a vanished context collides with modern conditions, producing misaligned behavior. The individual often recognizes the irrationality after the fact—"Why did I buy that?" "Why did I snap at them?"—"Why did I keep drinking?" but in the moment, autopilot ruled.

Recognizing these patterns is the first step toward Autognosis. By mapping signals onto daily experience, we begin to see the hidden code that governs behavior—not as fate, but as data that can be read, separated from, and ultimately redirected.

Civilizational Symptoms:

What plays out in the individual—the misfiring of obsolescent ancient signals in modern contexts—scales upward into the structures of civilization itself. Institutions, economies, and cultures are often not designed from first principles; they are emergent expressions of collective human impulses. When billions of people live on autopilot, their aggregated instincts shape nations and global systems.

Politics. The tribal instinct drives factionalism, splitting societies into opposing camps that behave less like deliberative democracies and more like rival clans. Loyalty to the group outweighs reasoned analysis of issues. Leaders rise not by offering solutions, but by amplifying fear and stoking in-group identity. The result is polarization, gridlock, and cycles of conflict that mirror the dynamics of prehistoric inter-tribal rivalry.

Economics. Scarcity and status impulses dominate consumer markets. Advertising leverages envy, insecurity, and hoarding reflexes to fuel perpetual consumption. Growth is celebrated as a measure of success, even when it depletes the very resources on which societies depend. Debt cultures flourish because present bias—choosing immediate gratification over long-term security—is built into the biology of decision-making.

Media. Attention, once directed toward immediate threats in small environments, is now hijacked by sensational headlines, curated outrage, and algorithmic feeds. The limbic system is easily captured by novelty, fear, and conflict, which become the currency of the information economy. The more reactive the signal, the more profit it generates.

War. Aggression, dominance, and territorial instincts scale from bar fights to global conflicts. Nations, like individuals, respond to perceived slights with escalation. The survival reflex of retaliation—once adaptive in face-to-face conflict—becomes catastrophic when amplified by advanced weaponry. The impulse that kept small bands secure now risks planetary destruction.

In each of these domains, the mismatch problem produces systemic consequences. Civilization is not failing because humans are inherently malevolent, but because the operating code of biology is outdated. Institutions mirror the limbic system, and reforms that ignore this substrate inevitably falter. Political revolutions, economic resets, and cultural renaissances repeat across history, yet the same cycles of corruption, collapse, and conflict recur. The signals remain unexamined, so the results remain unchanged.

This is the central diagnosis of Autognosis: civilization is an emergent limbic system, running on autopilot, mistaking instinct for wisdom. To evolve beyond this state requires more than policy or ideology. It requires individuals—at scale—who recognize the signals for what they are and reclaim the authorship of their actions

A Solution- Autognosis:

If civilization is caught in the grip of misfiring instincts, the question becomes: *what can be done?* At first glance, the answer seems bleak. We cannot edit millions of years of evolutionary programming with the stroke of a pen. The signals will continue to rise—fear, envy, anger, belonging—just as they always have.

But there is a way forward, and it begins not with suppression or denial, but with awareness. To recognize a signal is to break its spell. The moment you see anger not as "my truth" but as a limbic reflex, you gain distance. The moment you name envy as a status drive, you create the possibility of choice. Autopilot loses its grip the instant you realize you are on it.

The literacy of instinct is the foundation of Autognosis. It's not about erasing biology, but about learning to read it—like code scrolling across a screen—and deciding how to respond. From that literacy grows authorship: the capacity to shape one's actions by design, rather than by default.

The method is structured around five pillars:

1. **Recognition** – learning to notice and name the signals as they arise.

2. **Separation** – distinguishing between the impulse and the self who observes it.

3. **Redirection** – channeling instinctual energy into aligned, constructive outcomes.

4. **Reflection** – reviewing patterns over time, learning from both failures and successes.

5. **Design** – building intentional structures—rituals, habits, institutions—that encode chosen values rather than inherited reflexes.

These pillars will be explored at length in subsequent chapter. They serve as a compass pointing beyond instinct.

- Where the autopilot condition narrows choice, Autognosis expands it.

- Where mismatched biology creates dysfunction, Autognosis creates adaptability.

- Where civilization mirrors the limbic system, Autognosis offers a path to redesign the substrate itself.

In the chapters ahead we will examine this philosophy from multiple angles: as diagnosis, as practice, and as possibility. For now, let it be enough to say that liberation begins with awareness, and awareness begins with naming the signals for what they are. Autognosis is the practice of that naming, and the art of what comes next.

Now you can see how ignored obsolescent instincts can leave your behavior on reactionary autopilot. To see this clearly is both unsettling and liberating: unsettling, because it exposes how little authorship most people exercise; liberating, because by recognizing the autopilot we take the first step toward reclaiming the controls.

Chapter 2: The Hidden Code of Instinct

The Concept of Code:

Every urge, every surge of emotion, every reflexive choice is built upon lines of biological code—scripts written long before conscious thought evolved. These are not random quirks of personality. They are the algorithms of survival, engraved into the nervous system by millennia of natural selection.

Think of the human organism as a kind of legacy machine.

- Its hardware is the body.
- The user is the brain.
- And its operating system—the unchanged layer running beneath everything—is instinct.

Like lines of code buried deep within a program, these instincts execute automatically. They require no conscious permission or decision. Hunger tells you to eat. Fear primes your muscles to run. Envy sharpens attention toward rivals.

The metaphor of software is more than convenient—it is precise. A signal is an input ("threat detected"), which calls a function ("fight or flight"), which outputs a behavior ("attack" or "retreat"). The user—your conscious self—rarely sees the code directly. You only see the program being executed, from input to behavior. The instinct machine acts automatically, deciding for you.

The trouble is that this code is **archaic**. It was written for a world of small tribes, scarce food, and immediate physical threats. But the code hasn't been rewritten to fit the modern environment. Instead, it still executes faithfully, producing behaviors that once ensured survival but now create dysfunction.

Fear of exclusion that once kept you tied to a tribe now drives anxiety over social media validation. Status competition that once decided access to mates now fuels consumer debt and political demagoguery. The system is still running, but the environment has changed.

Understanding instinct as code strips away the illusion of mystery. It reframes behavior not as weakness or sin, but as execution. The system is not broken; it's outdated. And like any outdated software, it can be examined, debugged, and supplemented with new protocols.

This is the first step of Autognosis: seeing yourself not as an undivided self, but as a system executing code. Only then can you begin the work of separating author from autopilot.

The Core Drives:

If instincts are code, then the following represent their primary functions—basic commands that shaped human survival for tens of thousands of years. They are not inherently good or bad; each arose from real evolutionary pressures. In modern environments, however, they often misfire—triggering at the wrong times or in the wrong magnitudes. (This list is not all inclusive and emphasizes drives that most often lead to dysfunction. Pro-social impulses such as care, empathy, and play are equally real, but they fall outside the scope of this focus.)

Fear – The primal alarm system. Fear heightens senses, accelerates heartbeat, and primes the body for fight or flight. Once a safeguard against predators or enemy raids, it now surges before public speaking, job interviews, or deadlines—false alarms where the stakes are symbolic, not mortal.

Dominance – The drive to establish hierarchy and control. In tribal groups, dominance structured resource sharing and enforced order. Today it appears as office politics, authoritarian leadership, or bullying—hierarchies formed without survival necessity.

Belonging – The reflex to seek inclusion in a group. Exile once meant near-certain death, making belonging as vital as food or water. Now it manifests in conformity, peer pressure, and the anxious craving for digital "likes"—connection distorted into compulsion.

Reproduction / Attachment – The instinct to secure mates and protect offspring. It binds families and ensures continuity of life. In modern contexts, it can spiral into jealousy, possessiveness, and unhealthy dependency, straining relationships rather than safeguarding them.

Territoriality – The urge to defend space and resources. Once essential for securing hunting grounds or shelters, today it fuels property disputes, nationalism, and even road rage—territory reimagined through asphalt and borders.

Hoarding / Scarcity – The impulse to gather beyond immediate need. Stockpiling food or tools was a hedge against famine and long winters. Now it drives consumerism, compulsive shopping, and panic buying—overstuffed pantries in a world of abundance.

Curiosity – The drive to explore and learn. This instinct gave rise to fire, tools, and voyages into unknown lands. Today it fuels scientific discovery, but is easily hijacked into infinite scroll, clickbait, and novelty loops—endless curiosity without depth.

Status – The pursuit of recognition and rank. Once it signaled competence, securing allies and mates. Today it manifests in debt-fueled consumerism, workplace rivalries, and social media clout-chasing—status symbols detached from survival value.

Control – The urge to shape environment and reduce uncertainty. Adaptive when building shelter or managing risk, it now appears in obsessive micromanagement, anxiety over inevitabilities, or resistance to change itself.

Repetition – Comfort in the familiar. Routines once conserved energy and minimized mistakes. Now repetition calcifies into rigidity—clinging to habits, traditions, or dogmas long after they outlive usefulness.

Anger – A boundary-setting reflex. Anger once deterred threats and defended kin. Today it erupts in traffic, arguments, and online forums—disproportionate reactions where no predator is present.

Sadness – A withdrawal mechanism. Sadness conserved energy after loss and signaled need for support. In mismatched conditions, it stretches into chronic depression—withdrawal untethered from survival context.

Disgust – A protective filter. Disgust once shielded against toxins and disease. Today it extends into moral judgment and social prejudice—instinctive aversion misapplied to ideas, groups, or identities.

Shame – A social regulator. Shame aligned behavior with tribal norms, preventing exile. Now it often metastasizes into toxic self-condemnation or paralyzing anxiety—punishment disconnected from real threat of exclusion.

Thrill Seeking – The Inverted Alarm.
Fear evolved to keep us alive—an alarm system that primed the body to escape predators or fight rivals. But in the modern world, this circuitry often fires in reverse. Instead of avoiding danger, people chase it. Skydiving, drag racing, extreme sports, even reckless gambling—each hijacks the same neurochemical surge of adrenaline and dopamine that once fueled survival. The amygdala cannot distinguish between predator and parachute; the body reads *threat*, while the mind interprets *thrill*. What was once a mechanism to avoid harm has become a pathway for risking it, proof of how

instincts can misfire not only into phobias and anxieties, but into compulsive attraction to danger.

Taken together, these drives form the operating system of humanity. What was once adaptive has become misaligned in scale and context. Our instincts are not broken—they are over performing in environments that no longer match their original design. The point is not to demonize them, but to demystify them. They are not enemies, but code—code that can be read, redirected, and re-authored.

The Autopilot in Action:

Abstract explanations help us name the code, but stories make us feel it. Instincts don't whisper in technical terms; they grip us in moments. Below are a few glimpses into how ancient drives present in modern life:

Status – Envy in the Office

Maria had worked late three nights in a row to finish her report. At the morning meeting, her manager praised James—who had presented a flashier slide deck but had contributed less actual work. Maria felt a heat rise in her chest, a mix of anger and self-doubt. Rationally, she knew James's recognition didn't diminish her own competence. But deep in her nervous system, a status circuit fired: *your rank is slipping.* Recognition in the workplace carried no threat to her survival, but her nervous system responded as though she had just been pushed down the tribal hierarchy.

Belonging – Tribalism in Politics

On election night, Marcus scrolled his feed, heart racing as results trickled in. Every win for "his side" brought a surge of triumph; every loss, a flash of despair. He'd never met the candidates personally, yet he felt bound to them, as if their victory were his own survival. When a friend posted support for the opposing party, Marcus felt an instinctive jolt of betrayal—less like a disagreement, more like treason. The belonging instinct had been triggered: *my tribe vs. their tribe.* Politics became less about policy and more about primal loyalty.

Scarcity – Compulsive Shopping and Panic Buying

During a news broadcast about possible supply chain disruptions, Emma felt her stomach knot. Without thinking, she drove to the supermarket. By the time she got home, her trunk was filled with toilet paper, canned goods, and pasta—enough for months. She knew, logically, that the crisis was likely temporary and that stores would restock. Yet the scarcity circuit had fired: *take more now, or risk having none later.* What once kept her ancestors alive in lean winters now produced overstuffed pantries and empty shelves for others.

Reproduction / Attachment – Jealousy in Relationships

Daniel noticed his partner laughing at a text message. A flash of irritation spiked—irrational, even embarrassing. He trusted her. There was no evidence of betrayal. Yet his mind spun with questions: *Who was it? Why so funny? Why not me?* The attachment system had tripped its wire. What once ensured vigilance against rivals now strained modern intimacy. The emotion wasn't proof of truth, only proof of code.

Each of these moments seems personal, even moral: Maria feels wronged, Marcus feels righteous, Emma feels prudent, Daniel feels suspicious. Yet beneath the surface, each is simply the execution of ancient survival scripts. The emotions are real, but their context is misaligned.

This recognition reframes dysfunction: envy in the office, panic in the supermarket, rage on social media are not personal flaws but predictable outputs of legacy code. Once seen as such, they can be worked with—not by denial, but by conscious authorship.

This is the hidden code in action: reflexes tuned for one world, running unchecked in another. Seeing them through this lens is the first act of freedom.

The Layer of Illusion:

The most dangerous feature of instinct is not its raw force, but its convincing disguise. When a signal fires, it does not announce itself as *"biology at work!"*. It presents as reality. Fear whispers, *"this is dangerous"*. Anger declares, *"this is unjust"*. Jealousy insists, *"this threat is real"*. The mind rarely pauses to question whether the emotion reflects fact or merely echoes ancient code.

This is the **layer of illusion**: the reflexive belief that what we feel is what is true.

- A surge of **status anxiety** feels like proof that our worth is declining.

- A flash of **tribal hostility** feels like certainty that the other group is evil.
- A wave of **shame** feels like evidence that we are defective.

These are not moral failings. They are evolutionary echoes, the output of systems tuned to survival rather than accuracy. Our ancestors didn't need truth; they needed *advantage*. A false alarm that kept them alive was better than an accurate perception that left them vulnerable.

But in a modern context, this survival bias creates distortion. We don't just *feel* the signal—we become it. The identity merges with the impulse and becomes embodied when we say:

- "I am anxious."
- "I am angry."
- "I am worthless."

In reality, the signal is not identity. It is a message from an outdated operating system. Treating it as selfhood cements the autopilot condition—living as if every instinct were a command rather than a suggestion.

This illusion is reinforced by culture. Media, advertising, and politics exploit instincts precisely because they feel like truth. Outrage drives clicks. Belonging drives conformity. Scarcity drives sales. Entire industries are built on amplifying signals and packaging them as reality.

The first step toward liberation is seeing the illusion. Recognizing that the signal may be loud, but not necessarily accurate. That the feeling may be powerful, but not synonymous with truth. That "I feel" does not equal "I am."

"Mind over matter". Realizing that the impulse may not align with your desired outcome is how we turn impulse into data. Pain is one of the clearest, and possibly one of the most visceral demonstrations of how humans already interrupt primal signals with conscious choice. When someone "fights through the pain," they are deliberately overriding a powerful survival instinct because it conflicts with a chosen outcome. The common mantra *"no pain, no gain"* is an everyday example of this override: the body signals withdrawal, yet the mind insists on persistence in pursuit of growth. This is Autognosis in action—though unrecognized as such.

The example of pain override can serve as a benchmark for how the process works. "If pain — perhaps the most primal and urgent of all signals — can be bent toward chosen ends, then anger, hunger, fear, or envy can be just as deliberately engaged, reframed, and redirected.

This active override of instinct over outcome creates a gap in the automatic response system allowing us to consciously dictate our behavior. Autognosis begins in this gap—the thin but vital space between impulse and identity. It is here that awareness cracks the illusion, and authorship becomes possible.

Necessity of Intervention:

If the instincts that drive us are lines of code, then our first task is not to ignore them but to read them. Rather than attempting to erase them by willpower or ignore them into silence; they can be recognized, understood, and redirected. That is the intention of Autognosis.

Where the autopilot condition leaves us enslaved to instinct, Autognosis provides the tools for authorship. The process begins with three crucial practices:

- **Recognition** – Noticing when a signal has fired, and naming it accurately. Instead of "I am angry," one might say, "The dominance drive has been triggered." Language creates space. Naming dissolves the illusion of identity.

- **Separation** – Stepping back from the immediacy of the signal. The goal is not suppression but distinction: *this is a signal, not my self*. Like a developer examining a function, the individual begins to see the mechanism at work rather than being absorbed by it.

- **Redirection** – Channeling the energy of the impulse into constructive outcomes. Anger can become boundary-setting. Fear can become preparation. Envy can become motivation. The code is not destroyed but rewritten in application.

These three acts—recognition, separation, redirection—form the nucleus of Autognosis, later expanded into the Five Pillars that guide the full philosophy. They transform instinct from command into data.

The significance of this shift cannot be overstated. Civilizations, religions, behavior systems have tried to suppress, moralize, or ritualize instincts for millennia. Few have succeeded, because they never addressed the substrate problem: the code itself. Autognosis does not seek to deny biology but to place it in its rightful role—as one input among many, rather than the hidden driver of all behavior.

In the chapters that follow, we will map these signals more precisely, discuss tools for responding to them, and envision how individuals and societies might evolve beyond instinct. But for now, the key is this: the hidden code is not destiny. It is a starting point. And once seen, it can be rewritten.

Chapter 3. Civilizations as an Extension of the Individual

Civilization Instinct:

Civilization is often described in metaphors of machinery, architecture, or markets. We talk about the "wheels of industry," the "pillars of democracy," or the "invisible hand" of economics. But perhaps the more accurate metaphor is biological: societies behave less like machines and more like an extension of the limbic system.

Just as a brain is composed of billions of neurons firing signals that produce emergent patterns of thought and behavior, a civilization is composed of billions of individuals firing impulses, decisions, and reactions. What happens inside the skull also happens across society. The patterns of culture, politics, and economics emerge not from some master planner but from the aggregation of instinctual signals across millions of bodies and minds.

At this scale, entire societies exhibit the same reactive patterns as the individuals they're made of:

- **Fight or flight.** Nations rally into war after perceived threats or retreat into isolationism when overwhelmed—mirroring the organism's instinct to mobilize or withdraw.

- **Dominance hierarchies.** Just as primates establish pecking orders, societies stratify into classes, elites, and rulers, reproducing power dynamics on a massive scale.

- **Exploitation for gratification.** The same drive that compels an individual to hoard or dominate becomes systemic when civilizations channel labor, resources, and even entire populations into the service of elite appetites. Empires enslave, oligarchies extract, and consumer economies train citizens to feed collective cravings.

These parallels are not poetic flourishes—they're structural realities. Governments resemble executive brain functions, issuing top-down decisions. Markets behave like neural networks, optimizing for survival metrics such as growth and resource capture. Media systems function like sensory organs, amplifying signals of threat, novelty, or status.

When seen through this lens, the dysfunction of civilization comes into sharper focus. Just as a brain dominated by limbic reflexes struggles with impulsivity, aggression, or fear, a civilization dominated by unexamined instincts struggles with instability, violence, and excess. These civilization instincts are not rational, or deliberate, but reactive—their higher functions continually hijacked by their lower circuitry.

This concept helps explain why societies lurch from crisis to crisis despite advances in technology and governance. Civilizations, like the individual, are still running on ancient code.

Historical Patterns:

History is often written as the story of great leaders, brilliant innovations, or tragic accidents. But beneath the surface, civilizations rise and fall according to the same biological forces that govern individuals. Empires, economies, and cultures are not immune to instinct—they are *expressions* of it, magnified across millions of people.

- **Dominance Struggles and Imperial Collapse**
  The Roman Empire, for all its engineering marvels and cultural achievements, tore itself apart through endless contests of dominance. Emperors rose and fell in rapid succession, not because Rome lacked laws or armies, but because ambition, envy, and fear of rivals created perpetual instability. The same dynamic repeated in dynastic China, where court intrigues and succession battles weakened states from within. At scale, the **dominance** drive—so vital in primate hierarchies—becomes civil war and regime change.

- **Resource Hoarding and Economic Crashes**
  The Great Depression of the 1930s, while triggered by financial mechanics, was amplified by hoarding behavior. Banks pulled credit, individuals hoarded cash, and fear of scarcity collapsed circulation. Centuries earlier, mercantilist nations hoarded gold and silver under the illusion that stockpiling wealth equated to security, fueling wars and colonial exploitation. The **scarcity** reflex—once adaptive

in the wild—translates into systemic fragility when enacted by entire populations.

- **Tribalism and Genocide**
  The Holocaust was not an aberration outside biology, but an amplification of **tribal instinct**. The same us-versus-them reflex that bonded small groups for survival became, under the machinery of a state, justification for extermination. The Rwandan genocide of 1994 revealed the same pattern: in-group loyalty weaponized into out-group annihilation. Tribalism, once a shield against predators, became a license for industrial-scale violence.

- **Cycles of Overreach**
  Civilizations repeatedly collapse after periods of overexpansion—Athens in the Peloponnesian War, Spain's empire strained by colonial overreach, the Soviet Union under the weight of unsustainable competition. These are not random failures but expressions of the **control** drive: the impulse to extend dominance beyond sustainable limits.

Across cultures and eras, the pattern repeats. Instinctual drives—dominance, scarcity, tribalism, control—scale upward into wars, famines, collapses, and atrocities. The lessons learned are rarely sustained, because the substrate remains unchanged. New flags are raised, new constitutions written, but the code running beneath remains the same.

Civilizations, like individuals, cannot escape biology by ignoring it. They inherit its flaws wholesale, and history records the consequences.

Modern Case Studies:

The ancient forces that toppled empires and fueled wars have not disappeared. They have simply taken new shapes, embedded in modern institutions and technologies. Today's world, for all its sophistication, still bears the imprint of limbic reflexes.

- **Polarized Democracies: Tribal Belonging in Politics**
  In theory, democracy channels diverse perspectives into compromise. In practice, it often degenerates into partisan trench warfare. Political parties become surrogate tribes, offering belonging, identity, and certainty. The opposition is cast not as rival policymakers but as existential enemies. Social media intensifies the divide, rewarding outrage and loyalty signals with likes and shares. The instinct that once bound small clans against predators now fuels polarization so severe that consensus governance becomes nearly impossible.

- **Authoritarian Regimes: Dominance Instincts at Scale**
  The dominance drive, expressed in individuals as the pursuit of rank, manifests in nations as authoritarian rule. Strongmen leaders consolidate power, suppress rivals, and project

control to maintain their position at the top of the hierarchy. These regimes are often justified through myths of strength and protection—mirroring the primal allure of the alpha figure in primate groups. Yet, just as dominance hierarchies destabilize when challengers rise, authoritarian systems often collapse violently when the balance shifts.

- **Consumer Capitalism: Hoarding Reflex Industrialized**
  The modern global economy thrives on stimulating the scarcity drive. Advertising operates as a continuous reminder of what one lacks, while markets manufacture urgency through "limited-time offers" and perpetual novelty. Panic buying during crises—whether gasoline in the 1970s or toilet paper during COVID-19—reveals how thin the veneer of rationality is. What began as adaptive resource hoarding in the face of winter has become a permanent, system-wide reflex: entire economies predicated on endless accumulation, regardless of ecological or psychological cost.

Seen in this light, modern institutions are not divorced from biology but **extensions of it**. Democracies act out tribal loyalty tests. Dictatorships replicate dominance contests. Markets exploit scarcity impulses. Far from transcending instinct, our systems have **scaled it up**—magnifying primitive reflexes to global proportions.

The illusion of progress masks the reality: civilization still runs on limbic defaults.

The Substrate Problem:

At every turn in history, reformers have promised renewal. Constitutions are drafted, revolutions overthrow monarchs, international treaties outlaw war, and economic systems are reengineered. Yet the arc is familiar: stability gives way to corruption, unity fractures into factions, and progress stumbles into crisis.

So why do these reforms rarely endure? Because they operate on the **surface structure**, not the **substrate**.

The substrate is human biology—the instincts and impulses coded into us by evolution. Laws, institutions, and ideologies may be drafted with lofty principles, but they are carried out by individuals who remain subject to fear, envy, dominance, and tribalism. A constitution can declare equality, but if citizens and leaders alike remain status-driven primates, hierarchy and exploitation will re-emerge in new forms.

Consider a few recurring patterns:

- **Political revolutions.** The French Revolution sought liberty, equality, and fraternity. Within a decade, it devolved into authoritarian rule under Napoleon—a dominance reflex simply reborn under a different banner.

- **Economic reforms.** Post-crash regulations are enacted to stabilize markets, only to be eroded by greed and short-term incentives as memories fade. Scarcity and hoarding impulses do not vanish; they find new instruments.

- **Cultural movements.** Waves of social reform promise inclusion, tolerance, and compassion. Yet backlash arises almost immediately, fueled by tribal reflexes and fear of status loss. The instinct to protect the in-group does not dissolve in the face of moral appeals.

Institutions are like houses built on shifting sand. The architecture may change, but the foundation—our unexamined instincts—remains the same. Without addressing the substrate, reforms amount to repainting the walls while the ground erodes beneath them.

This is why history repeats itself with uncanny similarity. The forms differ, the rhetoric evolves, but the impulses driving collapse are constant. Until the substrate itself is examined and reshaped, reform remains cosmetic.

If civilization is meant to make us more civilized, then its first requirement is that we learn to distinguish ourselves from the uncivilized instincts we inherited as primates. The insight is sobering but clarifying: **civilizations fail not because they lacked better laws, but because they lacked better humans.**

This recognition has guided my own work. Every vision of a more ethical, less subjugated society

—one freed from the demand of survival labor—always circled back to the same obstacle: human behavior as the wrench in the equation.

Recursive Dysfunction:

Civilizations are not merely shaped by instinct; they *recycle* it. The very systems designed to regulate behavior—governments, markets, institutions—end up amplifying the impulses they were meant to contain. This creates feedback loops where unexamined instincts reinforce themselves, producing cycles of instability and collapse.

- **Leaders as Signal Amplifiers**
  When individuals with unchecked dominance drives ascend to leadership, their personal instincts ripple outward through entire nations. A paranoid ruler spreads fear; a status-obsessed politician fosters envy and competition; a tribal-minded leader pits groups against one another. Because leaders wield disproportionate influence, their internal signals become institutional policies, magnified through armies, bureaucracies, and propaganda. What begins as a single mind's reflex cascades into collective dysfunction.

- **Populations as Instinct Reservoirs**
  The masses, too, feed the loop. Citizens bring their own fears, desires, and tribal loyalties into the systems they inhabit. Democracies swing between extremes as voters react emotionally rather than rationally; economies oscillate in

booms and busts because investors follow herds rather than data. Institutions, in turn, must respond to these pressures, further entrenching the very behaviors they seek to regulate.

- **The Cycle of Corruption**
  Corruption exemplifies recursive dysfunction. A leader exploits power for personal gain (scarcity and dominance instincts). Citizens, witnessing this, lose trust and turn to self-protection and hoarding. Institutions weaken, making exploitation easier, which accelerates mistrust. The loop continues until collapse or revolution resets the system—temporarily—before the cycle begins anew.

- **Instinct as Self-Fulfilling Prophecy**
  Perhaps the most pernicious element is how instincts create the very conditions that justify themselves. Fear leads nations to arm themselves, which increases mutual suspicion, which confirms the need for more weapons. Status anxiety drives consumerism, which fuels inequality, which breeds even more status anxiety. Tribalism fractures societies, which reinforces the instinct to cling to one's group for safety. The feedback is recursive, a hall of mirrors where instinct feeds on itself.

The result is a civilization that not only inherits biology but becomes its *echo chamber*. Attempts at reform, without addressing the underlying code, are sucked into the cycle and reshaped by it. This is why history feels less like a straight line of progress and more like a spiral—repeating patterns at higher stakes.

Recursive dysfunction is not an accident. It is the inevitable outcome of building complex systems on an unexamined substrate. Until the substrate changes, civilizations will remain trapped in this loop.

Society Re-imagined:

If civilizations echo biology, then the solution cannot be written only in constitutions or treaties. These are surface codes, fragile overlays on the deeper substrate of instinct. To break the cycles of collapse, something more fundamental must shift: the operating system of the human mind itself.

This is the objective of Autognosis. Just as literacy once transformed individuals from passive hearers of stories into active readers of texts—reshaping economies, politics, and culture—so too can signal literacy transform us from instinct-driven actors into conscious authors of behavior.

- **From Reform to Upgrade**
  Instead of asking institutions to carry the weight of transformation, Autognosis begins with individuals. A society of autopilot minds will always revert to tribalism, dominance, and scarcity reflexes. But a society of authored minds—individuals who recognize, separate, and redirect their signals—creates a different substrate. Laws written by such people inherit deliberation instead of reflex, foresight instead of fear.

- **A Shift in Scale**
  One individual practicing Autognosis alters their relationships. A community practicing it alters its culture. A generation practicing it rewrites history. The lever lies not in top-down declarations, but in bottom-up rewiring: billions of micro-decisions, repeated daily, that slowly reshape the collective.

- **The Precedent of Conscious Evolution**
  Humanity has, in fact, upgraded before. Fire extended our diet beyond raw nourishment. Writing externalized memory, reducing dependence on oral tradition. Science institutionalized curiosity into systematic inquiry. Each leap occurred when a new layer of awareness and practice became widespread. Autognosis proposes a similar leap: an upgrade from reflexive instinct to intentional design.

This is not utopian fantasy but practical necessity. Recursive dysfunction will not end on its own; history shows us that. But by **changing the code at the level of the individual mind** societies can have a chance to stabilize and evolve.

Autognosis at scale is thus not merely a personal philosophy, but a civilizational imperative. If the limbic substrate has built the world we see, then a conscious substrate can build the world we need.

Part II – The Philosophy
Chapter 4. Autognosis Defined
The Name and its meaning

The word *Autognosis* comes from two Greek roots: **auto**, meaning "self," and **gnosis**, meaning "knowledge."

At first glance, it may sound like a familiar philosophical pursuit—knowing oneself. The Delphic maxim "Know thyself" (*gnōthi seauton*) has echoed through centuries of philosophy, religion, and psychology. Yet what Autognosis proposes is more radical and more mechanical: not merely knowing one's stories, traits, or preferences, but knowing the *code* beneath them.

Traditional self-knowledge tends to circle around identity: *Who am I? What do I value? What is my purpose?* These are important questions, but they operate on the surface. Autognosis asks instead: *What ancient instructions are running inside me right now? Which impulses are shaping my thoughts and choices before I even notice them?*

To answer that question requires a shift in metaphor. The self is not a fixed essence but a living program, composed of algorithms millions of years in the making. Fear, anger, desire, belonging—these are not mysteries or moral failings, but lines of biological code inherited from ancestors who survived by obeying them. Just as software runs silently until it crashes or loops, instincts run in the background, generating patterns we mistake for personality or providence.

Autognosis is therefore not about narrating the self but decoding it. It is the literacy of instinct. To practice Autognosis is to look beneath the theater of conscious thought and recognize the evolutionary scripts directing the play.

This framing has two crucial outcomes:

- It **dissolves shame**. Once an impulse is seen as biological code, it ceases to be a personal defect. Jealousy, rage, or anxiety no longer need to be carried as moral stains; they are recognized as signals.
- It **restores agency**. By seeing the code, one gains the option to step outside it—to separate, redirect, and rewrite, rather than obey it blindly.

In this way, Autognosis honors the old call to "know thyself," but extends it: to truly know thyself, one must first understand what the self is."

The Five Pillars Explained:

Autognosis is not a vague proposition to "be more self-aware." It's a structured practice with five interlocking pillars. Together they form a roadmap for moving from autopilot to authorship. Each pillar builds on the last, creating a cycle that turns raw instinct into intentional design.

1. Recognition — *Spotting Instinctual Signals in Real Time*

The first step is **naming the signal as it arises**. Recognition is about cultivating literacy: fear feels like a tightening chest, anger like heat behind the eyes, shame like an urge to shrink or hide. By attaching a label—*this is dominance, this is scarcity, this is belonging panic*—we transform what was once invisible into something observable.

Without recognition, impulses run silently, disguised as "truth." With recognition, they become objects of awareness. What was once "I am angry" becomes "An anger-signal is firing." That subtle shift opens the door to choice.

2. Separation — *Creating Cognitive Distance*

Once the signal is recognized, the second pillar is to create a gap between impulse and action. Separation means remembering: **I am not my impulse.**

This is not suppression, but reframing. A surge of fear does not obligate retreat; a stab of envy does not require sabotage. The signal is data, not destiny. Simple practices—pausing for a breath, naming the signal aloud, imagining it as a line of inherited code—help create this space.

Separation disarms the illusion of inevitability. It allows the individual to stand beside the signal rather than inside it.

3. Redirection — *Transforming Raw Drives into Aligned Actions*

Once distance is established, the raw energy of instinct can be harnessed. Redirection asks: *What constructive use can this signal serve?*

- Fear can become preparation.
- Anger can become boundary-setting.
- Envy can become inspiration.
- Belonging anxiety can become outreach.

The key is not to fight the signal but to **channel it**. Like a river diverted into irrigation rather than flood, the drive retains its force but serves a chosen end. Redirection turns instinct from master into servant.

4. Reflection — *Auditing Behavior and Learning from Patterns*

Autognosis is iterative. After the moment has passed, reflection anchors the learning. By journaling, replaying conversations, or simply scanning the day, patterns emerge: Which signals dominate? Which redirects succeed? Where does autopilot still reign?

Reflection is where theory becomes system. It transforms isolated moments of choice into cumulative self-authorship. Over time, reflection creates a feedback loop of awareness, adjustment, and refinement.

5. Design — *Encoding Values and Rituals into a Personal Operating System*

The final pillar goes beyond reaction into proactive design. If recognition, separation, and redirection are tools for handling signals, design is about shaping the environment in which they arise.

Here the practitioner encodes values into daily life through rituals, habits, and structures:

- Morning routines that anchor calm.
- Boundary rituals that protect focus.
- Community practices that cultivate belonging without tribalism.
- Personal codes of ethics written, reviewed, and lived.

Design ensures that when signals fire, they encounter a prepared system, not a void. It is the difference between improvising in chaos and rehearsing for mastery.

The Cycle of Practice

Together, the five pillars form a continuous cycle:

- **Recognition** sparks awareness.
- **Separation** grants freedom.
- **Redirection** channels energy.
- **Reflection** locks in learning.
- **Design** builds a resilient foundation.

This cycle is not linear but recursive, spiraling upward as each pass refines agency. Over time, the individual ceases to be a passenger on instincts and becomes an author of selfhood.

How It Differs from Other Traditions:

Autognosis does not emerge in a vacuum. Humanity has long sought ways to rise above its impulses, and many traditions have offered powerful tools. Yet each has its limits. To understand Autognosis, it helps to see where it converges with existing approaches—and where it breaks new ground.

Stoicism: Suppression Through Reason

The Stoics taught that passions are disturbances of reason and should be disciplined through rational detachment. When fear or anger arose, the Stoic ideal was to override them by appealing to logic and virtue.

- **Strengths:** Clarity, discipline, and an enduring sense of moral compass.

- **Limitations:** Stoicism often frames impulses as enemies to be conquered, creating tension between human nature and reason. Suppression, while stabilizing, leaves the underlying code unexamined. The signal is muted, not decoded.

Autognosis shares the Stoic commitment to virtue and agency, but diverges in its treatment of instincts. Signals are not tangible enemies to be conquered; they are simply data. Instead of suppression,

Autognosis advocates redirection—channeling drives constructively rather than silencing them.

Cognitive Behavioral Therapy (CBT): Thought Restructuring

CBT focuses on identifying distorted thoughts and replacing them with healthier ones. A fear of rejection, for example, might be challenged with evidence to the contrary.

- **Strengths:** Practical, evidence-based, highly effective for many psychological conditions.

- **Limitations:** CBT often targets *thoughts* rather than *instinctual origins*. A jealous thought is reframed, but the underlying reproductive or status signal may go unacknowledged. The symptom is addressed; the root remains.

Autognosis complements CBT but grounds it deeper: by recognizing that thoughts themselves are often surface narratives of buried drives. Rather than reshaping the story alone, Autognosis rewires the impulse beneath it.

Mindfulness: Observation Without Intervention

Mindfulness practices, especially from Buddhist traditions, emphasize nonjudgmental awareness. The goal is to observe impulses without attachment, allowing them to rise and fall naturally.

- **Strengths:** Cultivates presence, reduces reactivity, and dissolves over-identification with passing emotions.

- **Limitations:** Pure observation may leave the practitioner passive. While detachment can prevent destructive action, it does not necessarily transform the energy of the signal into aligned agency.

Autognosis honors mindfulness as a foundation for recognition and separation, but insists on a further step: redirection. Observation without authorship leaves instinct unchanneled. Autognosis pushes toward constructive design.

Jungian Individuation: Symbolic Integration

Jungian psychology frames instincts and archetypes as parts of the unconscious to be integrated into a whole self through symbolic work, dreams, and myth.

- **Strengths:** Deep insight into the richness of the unconscious and the value of integration.
- **Limitations:** Its symbolic and interpretive nature can drift into abstraction, leaving the practitioner without direct, actionable tools for daily signals. Archetypes are illuminating but can remain metaphorical rather than practical.

Autognosis resonates with Jung in affirming that instincts are not "bad" but meaningful aspects of our nature. Yet where Jung sought symbolic integration, Autognosis seeks functional reprogramming—transforming instinct not into myth but into practice.

The Unique Synthesis of Autognosis

What sets Autognosis apart is its biological grounding and practical reprogramming loop:

- It begins at the root—the biological substrate of human behavior.

- It treats signals not as enemies, distortions, illusions, or archetypes, but as code: inherited algorithms that can be read, understood, and rewritten.

- It unites observation (mindfulness), discipline (Stoicism), restructuring (CBT), and meaning (Jung), into a single framework. Then adds the crucial step of redirection and design.

In short, Autognosis is not suppression, not reinterpretation, passive observation, or symbolic integration. It is authorship: the deliberate construction of a self that acknowledges biology but is not bound by it.

Autognosis as an Operating System:

Most philosophical or therapeutic systems function like applications—useful programs one can "run" when the need arises. A person might meditate when stressed, use CBT techniques during anxiety, or apply Stoic reasoning in a moment of anger. These tools can be powerful, but they sit atop the same underlying platform: the human autopilot.

Autognosis takes a different stance. It is not an app; it is the operating system. A new system architecture that allows the user a new dimension of authority over their instinctual signals.

The Substrate of Choice

At its core, every human action—whether rational or impulsive—emerges from a substrate: the body's biological code. Instinctual signals like fear, dominance, and belonging are the default processes running in the background. Philosophical traditions and psychological methods intervene *after* these processes trigger behaviors, but the system itself remains unchanged.

Autognosis aims to upgrade the substrate itself. By training recognition, separation, and redirection into default responses, Autognosis doesn't merely offer strategies—it replaces autopilot with authorship. Once installed, the philosophy becomes the environment within which all other practices operate.

Ethical Agency From the Ground Up

Ethics often begins with abstract principles: "Do unto others," "Pursue virtue," "Seek the greatest good." But if an individual is still running on limbic defaults, those principles compete with obsolescent instincts. The result is inconsistency: lofty ideals undone by reflexive behavior.

Autognosis establishes a base layer of agency. By decoding and rewriting the impulses that drive us ethical frameworks can gain traction. Without Autognosis, ethics risks being ornamental—adopted in principle, abandoned in practice. With Autognosis, ethical principles are supported by an operating system that makes alignment possible in real time.

Compatibility and Integration

Just as an operating system supports many applications, Autognosis also supports—but does not replace—other practices. A practitioner of meditation, for example, finds mindfulness enriched by the active redirection tools of Autognosis. A Stoic gains a way to channel impulses rather than suppress them. A psychologist using CBT can anchor thought restructuring in a recognition of the signal beneath the thought.

The difference is orientation. These practices become applications running on Autognosis, rather than standalone fixes. The system becomes coherent, stable, and adaptive.

From Therapy to Design

Traditional systems often frame themselves as responses to problems: anxiety, anger, distraction, despair. Autognosis reframes the process. It's not only about fixing what goes wrong but about designing what comes next. Like an operating system upgrade, its goal is not crisis management but long-term stability, flexibility, and growth.

The resulting framework is where ethics, creativity, leadership, and community can be built on solid ground—not perpetually undermined by unaddressed biological defaults.

Autognosis, then, is not another tool in the kit. It is the architecture of authorship itself—the platform from which tools gain coherence, and the soil in which reforms can finally take root.

A Universal but Flexible Model:

Autognosis is not a philosophy bound to one culture, creed, or historical moment. Its foundation is biological, and **biology is universal**. Every human being carries the same evolutionary architecture—the same fear circuits, status drives, and belonging instincts—regardless of language, religion, or geography. What differs is how those signals are expressed, interpreted, and shaped by culture.

Because of this, Autognosis is inherently culturally adaptable. In one society, tribal belonging might manifest as nationalism; in another, as strict adherence to family honor; in another still, as devotion to an online community. The underlying signal is the same. Autognosis provides the literacy to recognize the signal beneath the cultural costume, making the framework relevant across diverse contexts.

Neuroinclusive by Design

Not every brain processes the world in the same way. Neurodivergent individuals may experience signals with different intensities, patterns, or triggers. A framework that assumes a "normal" mind risks excluding the very people who could benefit most.

Autognosis avoids this trap by focusing on signal literacy rather than rigid prescriptions. Instead of declaring what one "should" feel or do, it equips individuals to identify *their* signals as they arise. For some, fear may register as a racing heart; for others, as withdrawal. For some, anger explodes outward; for others, it implodes into silence. The philosophy's strength lies in its adaptability: the pillars of recognition, separation, and redirection are principles, not protocols. They flex to the needs of different nervous systems.

Teachable Across Life Stages

Autognosis is not limited to the academy or the therapist's office. Its tools can be scaled down for children—teaching them to name impulses before those impulses ossify into habits—or scaled up for leaders responsible for entire organizations.

- **Children** can learn signal recognition through stories and metaphors, giving them a vocabulary to decode their emotions before those emotions define them.

- **Adolescents** can practice redirection as they navigate the turbulence of belonging, identity, and status.

- **Adults** can apply reflection and design to build stable relationships, meaningful careers, and ethical frameworks.

- **Elders** can pass on wisdom by modeling authorship, showing how a life can be lived beyond instinct.

Because the framework is modular, it can be introduced in schools, workplaces, prisons, and even policy-making bodies. Its principles are simple enough to be taught broadly, yet profound enough to alter trajectories at every stage of life.

A Commons of Consciousness

Autognosis is not a closed doctrine but an open framework—a commons of consciousness. Each practitioner becomes both student and contributor, discovering new ways to redirect signals, new rituals of design, and new applications in culture. Like an evolving operating system, it improves as it is shared.

This flexibility is not weakness but strength. A rigid system may fracture under cultural or neurological diversity. Autognosis thrives precisely because it adapts. What holds it together is not dogma but the universal fact of biology and a shared desire to live by authorship rather than accident.

Chapter 5. Freedom is Built, Not Given

When we speak of *freedom* in these pages, it is not the language of governments or political systems. It is not about constitutions, ballots, or rights enshrined by law. The freedom at stake here is something more intimate and universal: the **freedom of self-will**. It is the capacity to recognize when an action is being pulled by inherited instincts and to choose otherwise. A society may guarantee civil liberties, yet its citizens can remain captives of their own impulses. Conversely, even in conditions of external constraint, an individual can practice authorship by reclaiming their responses. This is the freedom Autognosis names—the emancipation from autopilot that makes all other freedoms real.

The Illusion of Default Freedom:

We are told from childhood that we are free. Political systems are built on it, moral codes assume it, and religions either exalt or condemn us for how we use it. Yet when examined closely, most of what we call "freedom" dissolves under scrutiny. The unsettling truth is that the majority of our so-called choices are not authored at all—they are enacted by biological defaults long before conscious thought arrives.

Neuroscience provides the proof. Daniel Kahneman's framework of *System 1* and *System 2* illustrates how the brain operates in two speeds. System 1 is fast, instinctive, automatic—driven by the limbic circuits that evolved for survival. System 2 is slow, deliberate, effortful—capable of reasoning and long-term planning. But here is the catch: System 1 fires first, and often it fires alone. By the time System 2 engages, the body has already tensed, the words have already left the mouth, the decision has already been made.

Experiments reinforce this uncomfortable reality. In classic studies of "readiness potentials," neuroscientists found that the brain registers activity pointing toward a decision *hundreds of milliseconds before* the individual reports consciously making that choice. The implication is stark: free will as we imagine it—a sovereign self issuing commands from a throne of consciousness—is largely an illusion. We are often narrators of our behavior, not its authors.

This is what psychologists call the limbic hijack. Fear accelerates the pulse and narrows vision before reason has a chance to intervene. Anger floods the bloodstream with adrenaline before the mind can weigh consequences. Status threats and social slights trigger reflexes that evolved to keep us alive in small tribes but now steer boardrooms, ballots, and family dinners.

The illusion persists because the conscious mind excels at retroactive storytelling. After an impulse-driven action, the rational brain weaves a narrative: *"I chose to do that because..."* In truth, the "because" often arrives after the act. What feels like decision is more often justification.

This is not to say humans are automatons with no possibility of freedom. But it does mean that freedom cannot be assumed as the default state of being human. The default is autopilot—a sequence of ancestral algorithms running silently in the background, directing behavior in ways that feel like choice but are not.

To live without recognizing this illusion is to remain captive. To confront it honestly is to glimpse the possibility of something more: a freedom not inherited, but earned.

Freedom as a Discipline:

If freedom is not given by default, then what is it? In the framework of Autognosis, freedom is best understood not as a birthright, but as a discipline—a skill that must be trained, strengthened, and maintained like any other human capacity.

Consider language. A newborn is not born free to speak; the potential is there, but only through immersion, practice, and correction does speech become fluent. The same is true of literacy, mathematics, or athletic ability. No one assumes mastery of these skills without training. Yet when it comes to freedom—the highest claim of human dignity—we strangely assume it arrives fully formed.

Autognosis challenges that assumption. It argues that agency is constructed: built through repetition, reinforced through reflection, and encoded through intentional design. Freedom emerges when the fast reflexes of biology are interrupted long enough for conscious authorship to take hold. It is less a static possession than an active craft.

This reframing carries several implications:

- **Freedom requires work.** Just as muscles atrophy without exercise, agency decays if not practiced. A life lived without reflective pause will default to instinctual grooves, no matter how loudly one proclaims independence.

- **Freedom requires structure.** Paradoxically, discipline creates space for autonomy. Rituals, habits, and pre-commitments act as scaffolding that support higher-order choices when the moment of impulse arrives.

- **Freedom requires failure.** No one overrides instinct perfectly every time. The discipline of freedom is iterative: each misstep becomes material for reflection, each success a reinforcement of authorship.

This perspective also strips freedom of its mystique. It is not an abstract ideal, hovering above human experience; it is a concrete practice rooted in the body and brain. Every moment of recognition, every pause before reaction, every redirection of energy into a chosen path is a micro-act of liberation. Alone, they are small. Accumulated over years, they constitute a life authored rather than inherited.

Thus, freedom is not simply the absence of constraint. It is the presence of trained capacity—the cultivated ability to stand between signal and response and to write one's own script.

Historical and Philosophical Roots:

For much of recorded history, the idea of freedom has swung between two poles: innate liberty and inescapable determinism. Both shaped civilizations, and both, from the vantage point of Autognosis, miss a crucial middle ground.

During the Enlightenment, freedom was elevated as a natural inheritance. Thinkers like John Locke, Rousseau, and Jefferson framed liberty as self-evident—an essential human condition violated only by external tyranny. In this model, freedom is a baseline, and society's role is to protect it. The Declaration of Independence even enshrines it as "unalienable." Yet modern neuroscience paints a different picture: most so-called choices arise not from lofty rationality, but from automatic neural circuits firing beneath conscious awareness. If freedom were truly innate, why do humans so often act against their own stated values?

On the opposite end lies determinism—the belief that human behavior is entirely dictated by forces beyond control, whether divine decree, genetic encoding, or physical causality. Thinkers from Spinoza to certain modern neuroscientists have argued that free will is an illusion: we are biological puppets, our strings pulled by chemistry and circumstance. While this view acknowledges the power of biology, it denies the possibility of authorship altogether, flattening human aspiration into inevitability.

Autognosis cuts between these extremes. It begins with a sober recognition: biology is the default. Our instincts, biases, and drives are not chosen; they are inherited, scripted by millions of years of evolution. In this sense, determinists are correct—most behavior runs on autopilot. But Autognosis refuses to stop there. Where determinism sees inevitability, Autognosis sees potential for override. Through Recognition, Separation, Redirection, Reflection, and Design, individuals can interrupt biology's reflexes and train new patterns of authorship.

This places Autognosis in dialogue with traditions that emphasized discipline as liberation. Stoics spoke of training reason against passion, Buddhists of cultivating mindfulness against craving, existentialists of choosing meaning against absurdity. Yet Autognosis distinguishes itself by rooting this struggle directly in evolutionary biology and treating freedom not as a metaphysical puzzle but as a practical craft.

In short: Enlightenment liberalism assumed too much; determinism conceded too much. Autognosis insists on a middle truth—**freedom is neither guaranteed nor impossible, but conditional on practice.**

Training Autonomy:

If freedom is not a gift but a discipline, then it must be trained like any other capacity. Just as strength emerges from repeated exertion and memory from repeated rehearsal, agency emerges from the deliberate practice of overriding instinct. This is where Autognosis shifts from philosophy into method: its Five Pillars serve as a scaffold for building autonomy step by step.

Recognition: Interrupting Automaticity

The first step is simply noticing. Most impulses pass unseen, folded seamlessly into "I just felt like it." Recognition interrupts this invisibility. When the body tenses in anger or the mind spirals in status envy, pausing to say *"this is a signal"* creates the first wedge of freedom. Like catching a muscle twitch before it becomes a punch, recognition halts the slide into automatic action.

Separation: Establishing Distance from Impulse

Recognition alone is fragile unless paired with distance. Separation reframes the signal: *"I am experiencing anger"* is different from *"I am angry."* This linguistic and cognitive shift breaks fusion with the impulse. It is the difference between riding a runaway horse and watching the horse from the ground. The signal still exists, but its command is no longer absolute.

Redirection: Reclaiming Energy for Choice

Every instinct carries energy—fear sharpens attention, anger mobilizes the body, desire compels pursuit. Suppression wastes this energy, indulgence misfires it. Redirection captures the signal's raw fuel and channels it toward aligned ends. Fear becomes preparation; anger becomes boundary-setting; envy becomes aspiration. In this way, biology provides the voltage, but authorship determines the circuit.

Reflection: Building Meta-Awareness and Learning

Even successful redirection means little if forgotten. Reflection turns experience into instruction, embedding lessons in memory. By reviewing signals after the fact—journaling, auditing, or simply pausing at day's end—patterns emerge. Which signals dominate? Which redirects hold? Which fail? Reflection transforms isolated choices into a curriculum of freedom, each cycle teaching the next.

Design: Encoding Intentional Systems into Lasting Structures

Finally, freedom becomes stable only when designed into the architecture of life. Rituals, habits, and values are the code we write into ourselves. Design takes the insights of reflection and makes them durable: a morning ritual that preempts distraction, a value statement that guides decisions, a relationship boundary that prevents relapse into old reflexes. In this way, freedom shifts from occasional victory to systemic reinforcement.

Through these Five Pillars, autonomy is no longer an abstraction but a trainable craft. Each pillar interrupts biology at a different stage: recognition at emergence, separation at identification, redirection at expression, reflection at integration, and design at continuity. Together, they transform freedom from a philosophical debate into a repeatable practice of authorship.

Everyday Proof of Concept:

Soldiers: Mastering Fear and Reflex

Military training is, at its core, a systematic override of instinct. Left to biology, the body in combat defaults to fight, flight, or freeze. Heart rate spikes, vision tunnels, and fine motor skills collapse. Yet through repeated drills—marching under fire simulations, clearing rooms in endless rehearsals, responding to ambushes by rote—soldiers rewire their automatic reactions. Fear still surges, but training routes it into coordinated action rather than paralysis. When a soldier ducks and returns fire instead of fleeing, that is not biology—it is a constructed freedom born of conditioning.

Therapy: Reframing Emotional Reflexes

In clinical practice, freedom is forged on the emotional front lines. A person with panic disorder, for example, cannot stop the initial wave of adrenaline, tight chest, and racing heart. But through techniques such as exposure therapy or cognitive-behavioral strategies, they learn to recognize the signal, separate from its catastrophic interpretation, and redirect their response. Instead of fleeing a crowded store, they breathe, anchor to the present, and complete the errand. Biology screamed "escape," but practiced override allowed choice. This is Autognosis in microcosm: authorship gained, not given.

Education: Building Deliberate Attention

Schools, too, reveal the mechanics of freedom as discipline. A child's default biology prefers novelty, play, and immediate gratification. Sitting still to master arithmetic or language requires override. Teachers scaffold this process with structure—timed tasks, progressive goals, rituals of reward—that gradually strengthen the ability to focus. Over years, students internalize these disciplines, building the capacity to sustain attention on command. What began as imposed structure becomes an authored skill: the ability to direct one's own cognition against distraction.

These examples share a common thread: instinct does not disappear, but it is retrained. Soldiers still feel fear, patients still feel panic, students still crave novelty. The difference is that practice has encoded a second layer of response—one that suspends autopilot and inserts authorship.

This is the essence of Autognosis in action: the recognition that freedom is neither innate nor illusory, but cultivated. Each deliberate override is proof that the human animal can choose to become more than its biology.

The Stakes of Inaction:

If freedom is not trained, instinct reigns unchecked. The cost of inaction is not neutral—it is captivity. Individuals who never learn to interrupt their impulses live as passengers in their own lives, mistaking reaction for choice. The limbic system makes the call; consciousness merely narrates afterward, weaving justifications around what biology already decided.

At the personal level, this captivity appears as cycles of regret: the argument shouted in anger, the purchase made in envy, the relationship sabotaged by fear or jealousy. People wake the next morning and wonder, *"Why did I do that? I knew better."* The truth is simple: knowing better is powerless **without training** in doing differently.

At the societal level, the stakes compound. Millions of individuals running on autopilot generate collective patterns that mirror those same impulses—tribal politics, zero-sum economics, arms races, and ecological exploitation. Nations lash out like frightened organisms, hoard resources like anxious animals, and fracture into factions like rival clans. Without inner discipline, civilization becomes the stage on which unexamined biology writes its oldest scripts.

History is littered with the evidence: civilizations collapsing under greed, leaders undone by unchecked ego, populations swept into violence by tribal passions. In every case, reforms and revolutions attempted to fix the surface structures—laws, borders, systems—without altering the substrate. The result is predictable recurrence.

The inaction of the individual fuels the dysfunction of the collective. Each time we surrender to impulse without reflection, we strengthen the autopilot reflex. Each time we pause, redirect, and reflect, we strengthen authorship. This asymmetry means that progress is never guaranteed. Left alone, instinct will always win; only deliberate practice tips the balance.

Autognosis insists that the stakes could not be higher. In an era where technologies amplify our impulses at global scale—social media hijacking attention, markets magnifying greed, AI replicating bias—the cost of leaving freedom untrained is no longer just personal unhappiness. It is existential. **A species that cannot master its impulses risks becoming the victim of its own power.**

This is why freedom cannot be left to assumption or hope. It must be built, codified, and taught as a discipline—one life at a time, one choice at a time—until the weight of collective authorship bends the trajectory of history itself.

Chapter 6. The Engineering of Selfhood

The Myth of the Fixed Self:

"That's just who I am." Few cultural phrases are as misleading—and as limiting—as this declaration.

It masquerades as honesty, but in truth it is resignation. It reflects the assumption that identity is fixed, carved in stone by genetics, upbringing, or fate. This myth of a permanent, immutable self has long shaped human thought, appearing in everything from folk wisdom to philosophy, from religious doctrine to modern psychology.

The idea is seductive because it promises stability. If identity is fixed, then we can cling to the comfort of consistency: "we are who we are", and the burden of change is lifted. But what feels like stability is often captivity. When people insist they cannot change, they chain themselves to old patterns, no matter how destructive.

Modern neuroscience and psychology dismantle this myth. The brain is not a static organ; it is plastic, rewiring itself constantly in response to experience, environment, and intentional practice. Habits reshape neural pathways. Reflection strengthens prefrontal regulation. Trauma rewrites emotional responses, and healing rewrites them again. Identity is not a monolith but a process—a constantly shifting integration of biology, memory, and interpretation.

Even personality, often treated as a lifelong trait, is more fluid than commonly believed. Longitudinal studies show that traits like extroversion, conscientiousness, and openness shift over decades, influenced by life events, relationships, and deliberate effort. The "self" is revealed not as a singular essence but as an evolving architecture.

Psychology offers further evidence. Cognitive-behavioral therapy demonstrates that thoughts and behaviors can be systematically rewired. Mindfulness shows that attention can be trained to reframe experience. Behavioral economics reveals how context, framing, and choice architecture shape what we call "decisions." Taken together, these findings collapse the illusion of permanence.

Yet the myth persists, often reinforced by language itself. We say "I *am* angry" instead of "I *feel* anger." We say "I *am* anxious" instead of "I *notice* anxiety arising." Our grammar fuses identity with passing states, solidifying them into essence. Autognosis rejects this fusion. Emotions, impulses, and patterns are not the self—they are signals. The self is the author who decides how to interpret and respond.

Dismantling the myth of the fixed self is not an exercise in abstraction—it is liberation. It shifts identity from fate to project, from inheritance to authorship. To say "that's just who I am" is to close the door on growth; instead say "this is who I have built so far" and open the door to redesign.

Autognosis begins here: with the recognition that you are not a static entity but an evolving system. What you call "self" is not discovered—it is constructed. When we recognize ourselves as dynamic and malleable, we reclaim authorship not only over who we are but what we can become.

The Self as a System:

If the myth of the fixed self is false, what replaces it? Autognosis offers a different model: the self as a system, not a statue. Systems are dynamic. They have inputs and outputs, feedback loops, layers of function, and the capacity for upgrade. Your identity is less a portrait hanging in a gallery and more a living operating system, running code that can be patched, extended, or rewritten.

To make this concept tangible, we can think of the self as three interdependent layers:

- **The Biological Self — the Signal Generator**
  This is the base layer: the nervous system, hormones, instincts, and evolutionary code. It generates raw signals—fear, desire, anger, hunger, tribalism—without consulting higher logic. It is fast, reactive, and ancient. Like the BIOS in a computer, it operates beneath awareness, establishing the conditions under which everything else runs.

- **The Observing Self — the Interpreter**
  This layer receives and interprets the signals. It is the voice in your head that says, *"I feel nervous,"* or *"I want recognition."* It narrates

the impulses of the Biological Self, making them conscious. Crucially, the Observing Self can either fuse with the signals (*"I am angry"*) or separate from them (*"I notice anger arising"*). This layer is where awareness can interrupt autopilot.

- **The Ethical Self — the Author**
  This is the highest layer: the capacity for authorship. The Ethical Self decides whether to obey, redirect, or redesign the signals. It encodes values, principles, and chosen structures into behavior. In software terms, it is the custom operating system—the code written on top of the base firmware, capable of transforming hardware constraints into new possibilities.

Seen together, these layers form a living hierarchy. The Biological Self ensures survival; the Observing Self grants awareness; the Ethical Self enables authorship. Problems arise when the layers collapse—when raw signals leap straight into action without interpretation, or when the observer fuses with impulse and mistakes it for identity. This collapse is the essence of autopilot.

The system metaphor isn't meant to dehumanize but to illustrate through a tangible, relatable analog. Just as software can be debugged, modularized, and upgraded, so too can the self. Habits become subroutines; rituals act as automated scripts; reflection functions as diagnostic testing; values serve as source code. Every choice, practice, or redesign is a patch that changes the system's future outputs.

Recognizing the self as a system dissolves fatalism. You are not bound by your "nature," nor are you a blank slate. You are a layered architecture—part biology, part awareness, part authorship. And like any well-designed system, you can be maintained, refined, and improved over time.

Autognosis makes this process explicit. It equips the observer to see signals clearly, and it empowers the author to redesign responses. In doing so, it transforms selfhood from an accident of inheritance into an intentional system—one that evolves in alignment with chosen values rather than ancestral defaults.

Engineering the Self

If the self is a system, its construction can be described with the language of engineering. This isn't decorative metaphor—it's a practical lens for understanding how identity is built, maintained, and redesigned. Like any engineered structure, selfhood depends on foundations, codes, automation, diagnostics, and upgrades.

Values as Blueprints

Every structure begins with a plan. Values are the deep architecture beneath visible behavior—the "why" that holds identity together. Without them, life collapses into improvisations dictated by impulse.

- **How to Define:** Choose three to five core values (e.g., honesty, courage, compassion, growth).

- **How to Apply:** When facing a decision, ask, "Which choice aligns with my blueprint?"

- **Outcome:** Values guide long-term stability, ensuring the structure does not collapse under temporary pressures.

Principles as Building Codes

Design requires standards. Principles are actionable rules that enforce structural integrity. They guard against instinct overriding values in moments of pressure.

- **How to Define:** Translate each value into one or two non-negotiables. If the value is honesty, the principle might be: "I do not deceive, even when it costs me."

- **Outcome:** Principles act as guardrails. They prevent catastrophic failures of selfhood, much like safety codes prevent buildings from collapsing.

Rituals as Automated Processes

Engineers automate repetitive functions. For the self, rituals are engineered routines that reduce reliance on willpower and embed chosen values into daily practice.

- **How to Design:** Keep them simple, symbolic, and repeatable (e.g., three breaths before speaking in anger, nightly reflection, or a morning grounding ritual).

- **Outcome:** Once established, rituals become self-executing scripts, turning conscious choices into embodied patterns.

Reflection as Diagnostics

Every system requires monitoring. Reflection is the diagnostic tool of selfhood, catching where instinct overrides design.

- **Methods:** Journaling, end-of-day reviews, weekly audits, or trusted feedback.
- **Questions:** What signal arose? How did I respond? Was it aligned with my values and principles? What redesign is needed?
- **Outcome:** Reflection exposes drift, keeping the system evolving instead of decaying.

Design as Iterative Upgrade

No engineered system is finished; all undergo revisions. The same is true of identity.

- **Version Control:** Think of each shift in values, principles, or rituals as a new release—version 1.2 after a setback, version 2.0 after a transformation.
- **Iterative Upgrade:** Small, consistent changes compound into structural transformation over time.
- **Outcome:** This reframes change not as betrayal of a "true self" but as standard system maintenance.

Through these tools, Autognosis reframes identity as a living project. Instead of clinging to "who I am," the practitioner becomes an engineer of selfhood, crafting blueprints (values), enforcing codes (principles), automating with rituals, monitoring with reflection, and upgrading through design. The shift is radical but empowering: life stops being an inheritance to endure and becomes a system to craft.

Examples in Practice:

Abstract frameworks gain weight when embodied. The following examples illustrate how individuals, when equipped with the tools of Autognosis, re-engineer themselves—sometimes in the face of overwhelming biological and cultural inertia.

The Recovering Addict

Addiction is often framed as a moral failure or a purely chemical dependency. In truth, it is the rawest proof of instinctual autopilot: the dopamine reward circuitry hijacked, values overridden by compulsion.

- **Re-engineering in Action:** A recovering addict begins by recognizing the signal—urge as neurological echo, not identity. They establish principles such as, *"I do not negotiate with cravings."* Rituals are built around daily meetings, accountability check-ins, or evening journaling. Reflection uncovers triggers; design evolves as resilience builds.

- **Outcome:** Over time, the addict ceases to define themselves by the past compulsion. They are not "an addict forever," but a system under conscious authorship, running on new architecture.

The Leader Who Transforms Anger into Clarity

Leaders are not immune to biology; in fact, their roles magnify the stakes of instinct. Anger, dominance, and territorial reflexes often dictate decisions.

- **Re-engineering in Action:** A leader practices **recognition** by labeling anger in the moment. Instead of suppression (Stoic rigidity) or indulgence (rage), they redirect it: using anger as a signal of violated boundaries or injustice. Reflection converts the raw energy into strategic clarity—choosing principled action rather than reaction.

- **Outcome:** Meetings once marred by outbursts become arenas of steady presence. Authority grows not from intimidation but from trust. The leader's system upgrades from limbic dominance to intentional influence.

The Cycle-Breaker

Generational patterns—poverty, abuse, shame—often perpetuate because no one interrupts the autopilot script. One person, however, can alter the trajectory for descendants.

- **Re-engineering in Action:** The cycle-breaker confronts the inherited blueprint, often encoded in family rituals or unspoken rules (*"We don't* *talk about feelings," "You can't trust anyone"*). They rewrite the design: introducing new rituals (family dinners, open dialogue), adopting principles rooted in compassion, and reflecting on old triggers with distance rather than repetition.

- **Outcome:** Though imperfect, the system stabilizes into a new identity that children and grandchildren inherit—not by instinct, but by intentional architecture.

The Veteran Reintegrating to Civilian Life

Military training refines instinct into immediate reaction—fear becomes hypervigilance, dominance becomes command presence, tribal belonging becomes unbreakable unit loyalty. These reflexes, invaluable in combat, often clash with civilian contexts where nuance, patience, and openness are required.

- **Re-engineering in Action:** A veteran begins by recognizing the signal: the jolt of adrenaline at a slammed door is not present danger but a conditioned echo. Separation reframes it—"this is training, not reality." Redirection channels the vigilance into situational awareness rather than suspicion, the command impulse into mentorship rather than control. Reflection helps trace which responses serve in peace and which belong only to war. Over time, design replaces reflex with chosen protocols: pause, assess, act with intention.

- **Outcome:** The soldier does not lose their training; they integrate it. Warrior reflex becomes civilian strength, expressed as clarity, resilience, and leadership without aggression. Autognosis provides the bridge from battlefield code to consciously authored identity.

The Ordinary Individual

Not every transformation is dramatic. A parent who pauses before scolding, a worker who resists gossip, a teenager who chooses solitude over peer conformity—each is an act of engineering.

- **Re-engineering in Action:** Small rituals, anchored in reflection, reshape selfhood by degrees.
- **Outcome:** Over time, these micro-redirections aggregate into a life less ruled by impulse and more by design.

These stories reveal the same truth: identity is plastic, not fixed. Biology sets the default, but through values, principles, rituals, reflection, and design, individuals can rewrite their operating system. Autognosis provides the framework—discipline turns it into reality.

Risks and Responsibilities:

If the self is a system, then engineering it is not neutral work. Every blueprint carries consequences—not only for the individual but for those around them. Just as a poorly designed bridge endangers every traveler, a poorly designed identity can destabilize families, communities, and organizations.

Values Rooted in Fear

When fear becomes the blueprint, principles default to avoidance, suspicion, and control. Rituals calcify into defensive habits—hoarding, isolation, hostility. While these may provide a short-term sense of safety, the long-term system is fragile: brittle against uncertainty, corrosive to trust.

Designs Built on Dominance

A self engineered around dominance creates predictable failure points. Anger becomes the primary diagnostic, control the only ritual. Such a system may achieve power, but it remains unstable—dependent on intimidation, vulnerable to collapse when met with resistance. Like authoritarian states, these designs are outwardly strong yet inwardly hollow.

Over-Engineering and Rigidity

Some fall into the opposite trap: designing the self as a rigid machine. Excessive ritual, inflexible codes, or obsession with optimization can stifle adaptability. When reality shifts—as it inevitably does—such a system cracks. True engineering requires resilience, not just control.

The Problem of Borrowed Blueprints

Cultural narratives, ideological movements, or charismatic figures often offer prepackaged systems of identity. Adopting these without reflection may feel efficient, but it leaves the self externally authored. Such systems are vulnerable to collapse when the borrowed blueprint conflicts with lived reality.

The Responsibility of Influence

Self-engineering is never private. Every person's design ripples outward: children inherit parental rituals, colleagues absorb modeled behaviors, societies mirror the aggregate systems of their citizens. With this comes responsibility: the recognition that constructing the self is also constructing the world others must live in.

Key Point: Autognosis empowers authorship, but authorship carries weight. To engineer oneself without awareness of consequences is to risk building fragile or harmful architectures. Responsibility is not optional—it is the ethical counterweight to freedom.

The Promise of Systemic Selfhood:

If instinct is the default architecture of the human being, then Autognosis offers the possibility of redesign. What emerges is not a fixed "true self" discovered once and for all, but an evolving structure—dynamic, resilient, and authored with intention.

This view reframes life itself as a continuous design discipline. Just as engineers update systems, refine blueprints, and release new versions, so too can a person iterate on their identity. Each experience becomes data; each reflection a diagnostic. Failures are not endpoints but feedback—inputs for the next iteration of selfhood.

Identity as Ongoing Project

Rather than asking, *"Who am I?"* the Autognostic question becomes, *"What am I building?"* Identity is not a fixed noun but a living verb—an ongoing act of authorship. Every decision, every ritual, every reflection is a stroke on the blueprint of the self. Instead of clinging to the illusion of a "true" and unchanging identity, Autognosis frames selfhood as a dynamic project, continually versioned across time. Like an architect drafting revisions or a navigator updating a chart, the individual is always in the process of construction. This perspective releases the pressure to "find oneself" and replaces it with the freedom to design oneself

Resilience Through Design

A consciously engineered self is far more resilient than one left to default. Values chosen, principles codified, and rituals aligned with purpose create structural integrity that autopilot cannot provide. Just as a well-designed building can flex under stress without collapse, a self grounded in deliberate design can absorb disruption and adapt to uncertainty. Life will deliver chaos—loss, change, conflict—but the individual who has engineered their foundations does not shatter under pressure. Instead, they bend, adjust, and reorient while preserving their core. In this way, resilience is not merely endurance but the capacity to remain aligned with chosen values even in the storm.

The Gift of Iteration

The promise of systemic selfhood is not perfection but adaptability. Autognosis frees us from the illusion of a finished, flawless self. Each cycle of Recognition, Separation, Redirection, Reflection, and Design is an opportunity to release outdated code and install something more aligned. Like software evolving through countless updates, or ecosystems renewing themselves through seasons, the self grows by iteration. To live Autognostically is to embrace that the work is never done—and that this is the gift. Freedom lies not in arriving at some final version of identity, but in knowing that every moment presents another chance to revise, upgrade, and author anew.

The Ethical Horizon

If every person is a living project, then collective life becomes an interlocking architecture of self-designed systems. Families, organizations, and societies can evolve when their members are conscious builders. The long-term promise is not only personal authorship but cultural transformation: civilization as a designed system rather than a reflexive one.

Systemic selfhood is not a theory; it is a practice, a craft. Autognosis does not promise ease—it promises authorship. To live as a system-builder is to shoulder both freedom and responsibility, to accept that the self is never settled but always under construction. We do not need to be prisoners of inherited code. We can be authors of living systems and designers of our own humanity.

Part III – The Practice
Chapter 7. Recognition- Signal Literacy

What is Signal Literacy?:

Signal Literacy is the foundational skill of Autognosis—the ability to *read* impulses not as truths to obey, but as evolutionary messages to interpret. Just as literacy allows one to see letters and translate them into meaning, signal literacy allows one to notice an emotion, sensation, or urge and decode it as an artifact of biological programming.

In practice, this means that when a surge of anger rises, the literate mind does not say *"I am angry, therefore I must act."* Instead, it pauses to ask: *"What signal is this? What does it want? And does its message fit the present reality?"* The shift is subtle but profound: from inhabiting the impulse to observing it as data.

Neuroscience Foundations

Modern neuroscience supports this reframing. Research on affect labeling shows that naming an emotion reduces its intensity in the brain's limbic centers and increases activation in the prefrontal cortex —the seat of deliberation and choice. By labeling a signal ("This is fear," "This is status anxiety"), the individual shifts activity away from automatic reaction and toward conscious processing.

Why It Matters

Signal literacy is the baseline practice of Autognosis. The simple act of acknowledging a previously ignored autopilot signal as data makes it tangible. It's now something more real and relatable. Something that can be examined and evaluated. This practice illuminates the mismatch problem, fear triggered by credit card bills instead of predators, a lack of belonging from not enough social media likes instead of genuine group cohesion. Without literacy, we confuse evolutionary echoes for moral imperatives.

Signal Literacy does not suppress impulses; it embodies them. It doesn't deny or minimize their existence, it amplifies it. Shining a spotlight on the previously unseen. Signal literacy is the difference between being swept downstream by a current and being able to read the river's flow from the bank.

This skill is the genesis of Autognosis. Without the ability to recognize and name signals, the later practices—separation, redirection, reflection, and design—cannot take root. Awareness begins with vocabulary, and vocabulary begins with literacy.

The Core Map of Signals:

To become literate in signals, we must first map the terrain. Each signal is an evolutionary survival mechanism that still fires in modern life. Grouped together, they form functional clusters—protective, social, resource-driven, and growth-oriented. Recognizing them as families of instinct makes the map easier to navigate and remember.

Protective Drives

These instincts shield us from threats, toxins, and boundary violations. They are fast, forceful, and often disproportionate in modern settings.

Fear – Survival alarm. Once it primed us to fight predators or flee danger.

- **Cues:** racing heart, shallow breath, dread, looping "what if" scenarios.
- **Biological Basis:** Amygdala activation; cortisol and adrenaline release.
- **Modern Misfire:** Fear persists around abstract, non-lethal threats like deadlines or emails—constant alarms without predators.

Anger – Boundary defense. Mobilizes energy to confront threats or injustice.

- **Cues:** heat in the face, clenched fists, "this isn't fair" thoughts.
- **Biological Basis:** Sympathetic arousal, testosterone surge, reduced prefrontal inhibition.
- **Modern Misfire:** Outbursts in traffic, online rage, or hostility to slights far below survival stakes.

Disgust – Protective reflex against toxins and contagion.

- **Cues:** recoiling, nausea, curled lip, contemptuous thoughts.

- **Biological Basis:** Insula activation; autonomic gag reflex.
- **Modern Misfire:** Projected onto people and ideas, fueling prejudice and moral exclusion.

Sadness – Withdrawal and conservation after loss.

- **Cues:** heaviness, slowed movement, "nothing matters" thoughts.
- **Biological Basis:** Limbic activation, serotonin imbalance, parasympathetic slowing.
- **Modern Misfire:** Chronic depression, where withdrawal lingers without communal repair.

Social Drives

These instincts regulate belonging, hierarchy, and cohesion. They once kept tribes unified but now distort into polarization and harmful comparisons.

Dominance – Push to establish control. Structured order in tribes.

- **Cues:** clenched jaw, urge to "win," irritation at challenges.
- **Biological Basis:** Testosterone fluctuations; limbic aggression circuits.
- **Modern Misfire:** Office politics, authoritarian leadership, toxic competition.

Belonging – Need for inclusion. Exile once meant death.

- **Cues:** warm flush at inclusion, gut-drop at exclusion, "us vs. them" thinking.
- **Biological Basis:** Oxytocin release; mirror neuron activation.
- **Modern Misfire:** Nationalism, political polarization, online echo chambers.

Status Anxiety – Monitoring rank within hierarchy.

- **Cues:** chest tightness, envy, stomach drop when compared.
- **Biological Basis:** Serotonin regulation tied to rank; cortisol spikes with threat.
- **Modern Misfire:** Obsessive comparison, imposter syndrome, overwork to "prove worth."

Shame – Social regulator, preventing behaviors that risked exile.

- **Cues:** lowered eyes, shrinking posture, "I'm not good enough."
- **Biological Basis:** Overlap of pain and rejection circuits; heightened cortisol.
- **Modern Misfire:** Toxic self-condemnation, paralysis of expression, obsessive self-monitoring.

Reproduction / Attachment – Ensures procreation, pair bonding and care for offspring.

- **Cues:** chest flutter, longing, jealousy, fear of abandonment.

- **Biological Basis:** Dopamine, oxytocin, vasopressin systems.
- **Modern Misfire:** Obsessive jealousy, unhealthy dependency, commodified intimacy.

Resource Drives

These instincts evolved to secure territory, stockpile goods, and stabilize the environment. They often overshoot in abundance, producing waste and rigidity.

Territoriality – Defend space and resources.

- **Cues:** stiff posture, possessiveness, "this is mine" thoughts.
- **Biological Basis:** Limbic aggression, stress hormones when boundaries are crossed.
- **Modern Misfire:** Property disputes, nationalism, road rage, digital turf wars.

Hoarding / Scarcity Reflex – Stockpile for future shortage.

- **Cues:** restless grabbing, anxiety over "running out."
- **Biological Basis:** Dopaminergic reward loops; insula activation when facing loss.
- **Modern Misfire:** Consumerism, panic buying, clutter—shelves full while scarcity alarm still fires.

Control – Reduce uncertainty and stabilize environment.

- **Cues:** tense neck, shallow breath, "If I don't manage this, everything collapses."
- **Biological Basis:** Prefrontal cortex planning; dopamine reinforcement for mastery.
- **Modern Misfire:** Micromanagement, rigidity, anxiety over inevitabilities.

Repetition – Comfort in familiar routines.

- **Cues:** restlessness when disrupted, "this is how I always do it."
- **Biological Basis:** Basal ganglia habit circuits; dopamine reinforcement of familiarity.
- **Modern Misfire:** Addiction, ruts, clinging to tradition long after utility is gone.

Growth Drives

These instincts propel exploration, creativity, and expansion. They can lead to discovery—or endless distraction.

Curiosity – Urge to explore and learn.

- **Cues:** alert eyes, leaning in, "what's next?" impulses.
- **Biological Basis:** Dopamine release in anticipation of novelty.
- **Modern Misfire:** Doomscrolling, clickbait binges, compulsive novelty loops.

Together, these signals form the alphabet of instinct. Protective drives shield us, social drives bind us, resource drives stabilize us, and growth drives expand us. Each was tuned for survival in ancient contexts, but today they often misfire—commands from outdated code. Without literacy, they dictate behavior. With literacy, they become information: signals to be decoded, separated from identity, and redirected with intent.

Practical Checklist: Spotting Signals in Real Time

1. **Body First:** Scan for muscle tension, breath changes, or sudden energy shifts.
2. **Emotion Second:** Name the emotional tone (anger, fear, envy, desire).
3. **Thought Third:** Identify the story looping in your head.
4. **Cue Question:** Ask, *"Is this me—or is this my signal?"*

Signal literacy starts here: mapping sensations to signals, and signals to meaning. The more often this triad—body, emotion, thought—is practiced, the faster instinctual patterns become recognizable and interruptible.

Everyday Examples:

This concept comes alive when instincts are recognized not in theory but in the middle of lived experience. The following scenarios show how these drives surface in everyday life—often in ways so familiar that we mistake them for "normal" personality quirks or justified reactions.

Office Envy (Status Anxiety)

Maria opens her email and sees that a colleague has been publicly praised in a department-wide message. A flush of irritation rises before she can think. Her chest tightens, and a subtle thought creeps in: *"Why not me? I'm falling behind."*
This is not reasoned analysis but status anxiety firing—an ancient signal warning her of diminished rank in the tribe. Left unchecked, it could sour her relationships or fuel burnout as she overcompensates. Recognized, it can be redirected into motivation or gratitude instead of resentment.

Online Tribalism (Belonging + Anger)

James scrolls through social media and sees a post from "the other side." He feels his pulse quicken, anger mixing with a sense of loyalty to his own group. The content itself is secondary; the real signal is tribal belonging fused with aggression. His brain interprets disagreement as threat to identity.
Naming this pattern—*this is belonging and anger working together*—is the first step toward breaking the loop of outrage clicks and hostile comments.

Panic Buying (Hoarding / Scarcity)

During a news cycle about supply shortages, Emma finds herself loading her cart with more toilet paper and canned goods than she needs. She knows rationally that her pantry is full, but the primitive scarcity signal insists: *"Stock up, or you'll starve."*
Here, an instinct that once saved lives in famine now misfires in a supermarket economy, creating not safety

but waste and anxiety. Recognition turns the moment from compulsion into a conscious choice.

Territorial Arguments at Home (Territoriality + Control)

When Mark discovers his partner has reorganized the kitchen cabinets, his jaw tightens. He snaps, *"Why did you move my things?"* The conflict isn't about plates; it's a territorial reflex triggered by change in a shared space, amplified by a need for control.
Unexamined, it can escalate into unnecessary fights. Seen clearly, it becomes a chance to laugh at the absurdity of a prehistoric boundary reflex playing out in a modern kitchen.

Shame Spirals on Social Media (Shame + Status Anxiety)

After posting a photo, Lily notices fewer likes than usual. A pit forms in her stomach, and a voice whispers, *"They don't care. You're not enough."* What she experiences as personal inadequacy is really the shame signal entwined with status anxiety in the digital arena. Unchecked, this can lead to withdrawal or self-criticism. With literacy, she can reframe: this is not proof of worthlessness, but a miscalibrated instinct reacting to numbers on a screen.

Thrill Seeking – Chasing the Adrenaline High (Fear)

Eli clipped into his harness at the edge of the cliff, heart pounding. Logic told him that leaping into empty air with only a nylon chute was dangerous, but that wasn't the point. The rush came from the body's survival circuits firing at full volume—adrenaline flooding, senses sharpened, time stretching thin. His ancestors relied on this surge to outrun predators; Eli sought it out for recreation. The signal was designed to push him away from danger, but now it lured him toward it. What once kept the species alive had become a chemical thrill, addictive enough to risk life itself.

Each story illustrates the same principle: instincts still fire as though survival depends on them, even when the stakes are trivial or symbolic. Recognizing the signal doesn't eliminate the feeling, but it transforms it—from invisible puppeteer to visible input.

If signal literacy is practiced in this way, ordinary life becomes a classroom where the skill of authorship is honed for higher stakes situations.

Tools for Building Fluency:

Like any language, literacy requires practice. Awareness deepens not by reading about instincts, but by repeatedly engaging them in daily life. The following tools provide concrete ways to build fluency—the difference between recognizing a few words and becoming conversational in the hidden language of biology.

Journaling Triggers and Signals

Keeping a signal journal is one of the most effective methods of practice. Each time a strong emotion or impulse arises, the user notes:

- **What happened?** (the trigger event)
- **What did I feel in my body?** (sensations, tension, breath, heart rate)
- **What instinct might this be?** (fear, status anxiety, shame, etc.)
- **How did I respond?** (reaction, suppression, redirection)

Over time, the journal reveals patterns. Readers may discover that certain contexts—meetings, family interactions, social media—consistently spark the same instincts. This self-generated dataset makes the invisible visible.

Body Scans to Locate Physical Tension

Instincts speak through the body before the mind. A tight jaw, clenched fists, shallow breath—these are the earliest signals. Practicing daily body scans helps attune awareness to these cues.

A simple routine:

1. Sit quietly for 2–3 minutes.
2. Bring attention slowly from the crown of the head to the toes.
3. At each point, ask: *"What do I notice? Tension, warmth, hollowness?"*
4. Note sensations without judgment.

With repetition, users learn to catch signals earlier, before they spiral into reaction.

"Name It to Tame It" (Affect Labeling)

This technique, backed by neuroscience, reduces emotional intensity by translating raw feeling into words. The practice is simple: when a strong signal arises, label it out loud or silently—*"This is fear." "This is shame." "This is territoriality."*

The act of naming shifts activity from the amygdala (emotional center) to the prefrontal cortex (reasoning center). It does not erase the signal but weakens its grip, creating a window for conscious choice.

Signal Cards or Prompts for Quick Reference

To reinforce literacy in real-world contexts, users can create or carry "signal cards"—small reminders listing the core instincts and their cues. For example:

- **Fear:** tight chest, urge to retreat.
- **Status Anxiety:** envy, comparison, rumination.
- **Belonging:** relief with group approval, discomfort with dissent.
- **Shame:** sinking stomach, self-directed attack.

Flipping through the cards in moments of intensity provides a fast diagnostic tool. Some readers adapt this into digital reminders or phone wallpapers to keep the practice near at hand.

Building the Muscle of Recognition

Each of these tools strengthens the capacity to notice, name, and interpret instincts in real time. Like training any skill—playing piano, learning a sport—the key is repetition. Signal literacy can become second nature when practiced consistently.

By adopting these tools, users begin to shift from being swept along by unconscious impulses to observing them as structured, recognizable signals. This is the bedrock upon which separation, redirection, and deeper Autognosis practices are built.

The Challenge of Overlap:

Signals rarely arrive one at a time. In real life, instincts stack, blend, and mask one another—creating composite states that are easy to misread. Literacy requires nuance: not "which single signal is this?" but "which signals are co-active, and which one is primary?"

Common Blends (with typical outputs)

- **Fear + Dominance → Aggression.** Threat arousal (fear) fuels a control move (dominance): snapping, posturing, escalation.

- **Belonging + Shame → Conformity/Self-silencing.** Need to stay "in" plus fear of exposure yields agreeableness at the cost of integrity.

- **Scarcity + Control → Micromanagement.** Anticipated loss drives grasping; control tightens procedures, trust collapses.

- **Status Anxiety + Curiosity → Clout-chasing.** Novelty seeking steered by rank concerns: headline skimming, performative takes.

- **Disgust + Tribal Belonging → Dehumanization.** Purity reflex applied to out-groups; empathy drops, moral exclusion rises.

- **Sadness + Belonging → Nostalgia Loops.** Loss signal seeks group warmth; idealized past inhibits adaptation.

- **Shame + Anger → Blame-Shifting.** Exposure pain converts into attack to deflect attention.

Primary vs. Secondary Signals

Many "loud" behaviors are **secondary covers** over a quieter primary signal:

- Anger often **covers fear or shame** ("If I look strong, I won't look vulnerable").

- Control often **covers scarcity** ("If I manage every variable, nothing will be taken").

- Conformity often **covers belonging panic** ("If I dissent, I'll be cast out").

Ask: **"What would remain if I removed the top layer?"**
If the anger cooled, would fear of loss still be there? If

the perfectionism softened, would scarcity anxiety remain?

Disambiguation Tools (how to tell blends apart)

Function Test (What is it trying to do for me?)

- Protect from **harm** → likely fear primary.
- Protect **rank/face** → likely status/shame.
- Restore **order** → likely control/dominance.
- Regain **belonging** → likely belonging/shame.

Somatic Signature (Where is it in the body?)

- **Chest/heart rate**: fear; **jaw/hands heat**: anger/dominance;
- **Stomach drop**: shame/status; **throat lump/heaviness**: sadness;
- **Nausea/curling lip**: disgust.
  Note the **first** sensation—primary signals tend to fire earliest.

Time Course (Spike vs. Wave)

- **Fast spikes** (milliseconds–seconds): fear, anger, disgust.
- **Slow waves** (minutes–hours): sadness, shame, status anxiety.
  A spike followed by a wave suggests a

primary fast signal with a secondary mood.

Context Diagnostic (Where did it arise?)

- **Audience present?** Status/belonging likely.
- **Resource at stake?** Scarcity/territoriality.
- **Boundary crossed?** Anger/dominance.
- **Ambiguity/high variance?** Control.

Language Audit (The story it tells)

- "They'll **think** I'm…" → shame/status.
- "What if we **run out**?" → scarcity.
- "They **can't** do that to me." → dominance.
- "This is **dangerous**." → fear.

A Quick "Stack Decode" Protocol

Name the top layer (the obvious one): "Anger is here."

Probe for the base with three questions:

- *What am I afraid will happen?* (fear)
- *What belonging or status feels at risk?* (belonging/shame/status)
- *What resource/control feels threatened?* (scarcity/control/territory)

Prioritize by first sensation + function.

Redirect by layer:

- Primary **fear** → safety/plan.
- Primary **shame** → values/repair.
- Primary **scarcity** → inventory/reality-check.
- Primary **dominance** → boundary with calm.

Practice Drills

- **Two-Label Rule:** In tense moments, name **at least two** active signals ("fear + dominance"). This reduces over-simplification.
- **Peel-Back in Writing:** Journal the incident three times, each pass naming what sits **under** the prior label.
- **Role Flip:** Ask a trusted other to label what they see; outside observers often spot the **covered** signal.

Why Nuance Matters

Reduction ("it's just anger") keeps autopilot intact. Nuance exposes the mechanism and opens more precise redirects. An aggression episode handled as fear-primary leads to planning and reassurance; handled as dominance-primary it leads to firm, ethical boundaries. The difference changes outcomes.

From knowledge to Action:

But recognition alone—even nuanced recognition—is not enough. To see a drive is to shine a flashlight on the hidden machinery of the self, yet the light does not turn the gears. Without another step, recognition can even become paralyzing: a person sees their impulses clearly, but still feels swept along by them.

This is why Autognosis insists on **Separation**. Awareness must be paired with distance. The moment between "I feel it" and "I am it" is the hinge on which freedom turns. Before signals can be redirected, they must be uncoupled from identity. Recognition names the signal; Separation creates the space to choose.

Chapter 8 – Separation-You Are Not Your Impulse

A thought is not an action. A feeling is not a fact. An urge is not a command.

Separation is the second pillar of Autognosis. It is the disciplined ability to notice a biological signal without fusing with it. Where Recognition says, "This is fear," Separation says, "This is fear, and I am not fear." It is the pause between limbic spark and conscious authorship—the moment in which the self steps outside its automatic programming.

Importance of Separation:

Signals fire fast. By the time you feel the surge of anger, shame, or fear, the limbic system has already launched its chemical cascade. Unless you have trained to pause, behavior follows reflex. This is why so many people say, "I don't know what came over me." Something *did* come over them—the biology of a survival algorithm misfiring in modern life.

Without Separation, Recognition can backfire. Seeing an impulse clearly but still obeying it can make people feel powerless: *I knew I was overreacting, but I couldn't stop myself.* This is the trap of identity fusion. When we equate "I am angry" with "I must act angrily," the signal becomes outcome.

Separation interrupts this fusion. It does not deny the anger, fear, or shame—it reframes it. *Anger is present, but I remain larger than anger. Fear is firing, but I am not fear.* This shift in language and perspective cracks open the smallest but most powerful space: the ability to choose. Every redirect, every reflection, every personal design depends on this gap. Without it, Autognosis collapses into mere awareness. With separation, awareness becomes agency.

Scientific Basis:

The case for Separation is not only philosophical—it is neurological. The amygdala, the brain's alarm bell, reacts in under 200 milliseconds. The prefrontal cortex, responsible for deliberate reasoning, requires several hundred milliseconds more. Separation gives the cortex the time it needs to weigh in.

Psychological research confirms this mechanism. In Acceptance and Commitment Therapy (ACT), "cognitive defusion" is a central practice. Clients are taught to insert a phrase—"I am having the thought that…"—to unhook from the thought itself. Studies show this reduces emotional intensity and increases flexibility.

Ancient philosophy discovered the same principle without fMRI. The Stoics called it *prohairesis*—the will to choose one's response. Epictetus taught that between what happens to us and how we respond lies an interval, and in that interval resides freedom. Separation is simply the modern articulation of that insight: a trainable skill to extend the gap between stimulus and response.

Practices of Separation:

How does one learn to step outside their signals? The answer is practice, not theory.

Breathwork

A single slow exhale lengthens the pause. It calms the sympathetic nervous system, signals safety to the body, and buys a few precious seconds. In those seconds, the cortex can re-engage.

Labeling

Words matter. Saying "I am angry" fuses self with signal. Saying "Anger is present" or "Shame is firing" reframes the experience as an event in the mind, not an identity. This small shift in wording is decisive in effect.

Observer Shift

Visualize watching yourself from outside—standing behind your own shoulder or floating above the scene. Or imagine yourself as the operator seated at the controls inside the machine that is your body. The signal becomes part of the system's readout, not the author of your actions. You are not the surge of anger or fear—you are the one noticing it on the dashboard. You can watch the gauges spike, see the levers twitch, and still thoughtfully decide how to steer. From this vantage, the signal is visible as part of the story, not the author of it.

Somatic Mapping

Signals often announce themselves in the body first: tension in the jaw, a stomach drop, a racing heart. Naming these sensations—*heat in the chest, tightness in the throat*—turns vague emotion into observable data. This data creates distance.

Separation does not silence the signal. It makes it graspable. You go from being lost in the storm to standing under shelter, observing the rain and thunder pass by.

Drills and Tools:

The Three-Second Rule

Before reacting—especially in conflict—count a slow three. This interrupts the reflex arc. Three seconds can feel like an eternity to the limbic system, but it is all the time the cortex needs to intervene.

Defusion Cards

Write down your common triggers on note cards —"fear of loss," "status threat," "scarcity." When the trigger arises, pull out the card and read: *This is just the program firing.* The act of naming it interrupts its authority.

Role-Play Rehearsal

Separation is easier to practice in low-stakes environments. Use daily inconveniences—traffic, minor annoyances, social slights—as training ground. If you can notice and detach there, you will be prepared when the stakes are higher.

Somatic Anchors

Choose a small physical gesture that signals Separation: touching your wrist, pressing your fingertips together, or placing a hand on your chest. Condition yourself so the gesture cues the shift into observer mode.

These drills may seem simple, even juvenile, but their effect compounds. Each pause builds the muscle of distance. Over time, the practice becomes reflexive — the tools shift from something you reach for to something you embody.

Developmental Scaling:

Children

Young learners can be taught that "feelings are visitors." They come, they stay a while, and they leave. Drawing feelings as characters who visit the "house of the self" helps externalize emotion without suppression.

Adolescents

Teenagers benefit from writing prompts: "I am having the thought that…" or "Shame is saying…" Journaling in this style creates early practice of cognitive defusion.

Adults

Adults can create protocols for recurring triggers: *When I feel dismissed, I say aloud, 'This is not me. This is the program.'* Externalizing the script preserves dignity in moments where autopilot would otherwise take over.

Separation is scalable because it is universal. The human brain, whether at age six or sixty, responds to the same signals. What changes is the language and ritual used to create distance.

Outcome:

Separation does not erase signals—it reframes them as material. You are not swallowed by fear, shame, or anger; you are the one holding them at arm's length, deciding what to do next. It allows you to observe the why before intentionally directing your behavior. Recognition illuminates the code. Separation unhooks you from it. From here Redirection towards self authorship can begin.

Chapter 9. The Redirection Toolkit

Why Redirection Matters:

As we've seen Separation is powerful, but still incomplete. To see and separate instincts as they rise within us is to pause the autopilot, yet without the next step that pause can quickly collapse into one of two extremes: **suppression** or **explosion**.

- **Suppression** occurs when a person notices their anger, envy, or fear and forces it underground. The energy is buried but not neutralized, often resurfacing later as stress, illness, or misplaced hostility.

- **Explosion** is the opposite extreme: the impulse is given full reign, acted out in ways that may feel relieving in the moment but destructive in outcome—arguments, outbursts, addictions, broken trust.

Neither option creates freedom. Suppression chains us to hidden tensions, while explosion chains us to regret. Both represent a failure to work *with* the instinct's energy.

Redirection is the transformation.

Once impulses are observed and detached they can be harnessed as fuel and be transformed. The raw energy of anger can power assertiveness; the pang of jealousy can become a cue for growth; fear can sharpen preparation rather than paralyze.

Redirection is therefore not a denial of biology but an upgrade of it. It takes the evolutionary signal—"move, act, secure, survive"—and translates it into motion aligned with chosen values. In this way, Autognosis transforms instincts from liabilities into assets.

The Principles of Redirection:

Impulse energy is fuel, not fate.

Every instinct carries energy—adrenaline, urgency, intensity. The mistake is assuming that because the energy points in one direction, we must follow it. In truth, this energy is neutral until applied. Anger can destroy or defend. Desire can exploit or create intimacy. Fear can freeze or focus. The power of Autognosis lies in *decoupling the energy from the default behavior* and reapplying it where it serves.

The goal is alignment, not denial.

Suppression starves the signal; indulgence drowns in it. Redirection seeks alignment—taking the evolutionary purpose of the signal (to protect, to secure, to bond) and matching it with the individual's consciously chosen values. For example: the territorial urge is about security. Alignment might mean securing one's boundaries through calm dialogue, not escalating conflict. The signal is acknowledged, honored, and translated into constructive action.

Alternatives must be preloaded before the crisis moment.

In the heat of anger or jealousy, the limbic system outruns deliberation. Redirection succeeds only if alternative pathways are rehearsed in advance. Soldiers drill until reactions are automatic; athletes visualize responses before competition. In the same way, an individual must preload constructive redirects —walking away, breathing, journaling, calling a trusted friend—so that in the moment of crisis the body has a **ready-made alternative circuit**. Without this preparation, the old code runs by default.

Redirection Models:

Decode → Match → Channel framework:

- Decode the impulse (What does it want to do for me?).

- Match the function (What's a value-aligned way to meet that need?).

- Channel the energy (How can I use this drive as momentum?).

At its core, redirection is not guesswork but a repeatable process. The **Decode → Match → Channel** framework provides a simple map for transforming instinct into authorship:

- **Decode the impulse (What does it want to do for me?).**
  Every instinct has a hidden purpose. Anger often seeks to restore safety. Envy signals a longing for status or recognition. Fear protects against

loss. By asking, *"What is this signal trying to accomplish?"*, the raw emotion is translated into information. Decoding reframes the impulse from an enemy into a messenger.

- **Match the function (What's a value-aligned way to meet that need?).**
Once the message is understood, the next step is alignment. If anger seeks safety, perhaps safety can be built by calmly stating boundaries rather than lashing out. If envy seeks recognition, the aligned action may be developing one's skills or giving credit to others, rather than tearing someone down. Matching is about honoring the *function* of the instinct while rejecting its outdated *method*.

Channel the energy (How can I use this drive as momentum?).

The final step is action. Energy must go somewhere—if it is not channeled, it stagnates or explodes. Fear can become focus through preparation. Sadness can become art through expression. Desire can become motivation through goal-setting. The channeling step converts raw biological fuel into motion that builds rather than erodes.

With practice, this three-step model is not only practical but repeatable. It becomes an *automatic translator*—a way of intercepting instinct and converting it into choice, moment by moment.

Practical Toolkit:

- Redirect scripts (e.g., "I feel jealous → this is about insecurity → I can clarify my values and connect instead").
- Physical redirects (walks, breathing exercises, cold water immersion).
- Cognitive redirects (reframing questions, journaling prompts).
- Social redirects (seeking connection, offering help, collaborative problem-solving).
- Creative redirects (art, music, writing as energy outlets).

Redirection becomes real when tools are simple, memorable, and immediately deployable. The following strategies provide a range of entry points—mental, physical, social, and creative—so that instinctual energy can be transmuted rather than suppressed or indulged.

Redirect Scripts
Quick mental phrases act like interrupts, breaking the cycle of automatic reaction:

- *"I feel jealous → this is about insecurity → I can clarify my values and connect instead."*
- *"I feel anger → this is about safety → I can set a boundary instead of explode."*
- *"I feel shame → this is about belonging → I can seek connection rather than hide."*

These micro-scripts create a bridge between recognition and constructive motion.

Physical Redirects

Instincts live in the body, and moving energy physically is often the fastest way to release pressure:

- A brisk walk to metabolize adrenaline.
- Deep breathing to restore parasympathetic balance.
- Cold water immersion to reset nervous system overwhelm.
- Stretching or exercise to channel restless energy.

Cognitive Redirects

When the mind is spiraling, redirection requires new frames of interpretation:

- Reframing questions: *"What else could this mean?"* or *"What value of mine is being touched here?"*
- Journaling prompts to untangle thought loops.
- Listing constructive alternatives before the moment of crisis.
  Cognitive redirection is like debugging faulty code—locating the glitch and rewriting it in real time.

Social Redirects

Because many instincts relate to belonging and status, redirection often requires interaction:

- Seeking connection rather than isolation.

- Offering help to counter envy or rivalry.
- Collaborative problem-solving instead of dominance struggles.
  The social sphere is both the trigger and the cure; redirection here restores alignment with shared values.

Creative Redirects

Some signals resist logic and demand expression:

- Transforming sadness into poetry, painting, or song.
- Channeling anger into drumming, dance, or physical art forms.
- Using curiosity to fuel innovation, tinkering, or storytelling.
  Creative outlets transmute raw signal energy into beauty, meaning, or contribution.

Together, these tools form a multi-modal toolkit. Each person will naturally gravitate toward some over others, but mastery comes from rehearsing multiple options. This ensures that when the moment of instinct arrives, there is always a ready outlet for transformation.

Case Studies and Vignettes:

Redirection is not an abstract skill—it comes alive in the everyday moments where instinct collides with choice. The following vignettes illustrate how raw impulses, if left unchecked, risk harm or stagnation, but when redirected, become fuel for growth.

Anger → Boundary-Setting
Scenario: A manager receives yet another late-night message from a colleague demanding immediate action. The body tenses, pulse quickens, and an angry retort forms.
Old path: Sending a heated reply, escalating conflict.
Redirection: Pausing to decode: *"This anger is signaling that my boundaries are being crossed."* The manager drafts a calm but firm response the next morning, setting clear limits on communication hours. Anger becomes not destruction, but a catalyst for self-respect.

Fear → Planning
Scenario: A student faces mounting anxiety before an important exam. Fear floods the system: shallow breaths, racing heart, spiraling thoughts of failure.
Old path: Freezing, procrastination, avoidance.
Redirection: Recognizing the fear as a survival signal: *"This is my body asking me to prepare."* Instead of panic, the student channels the energy into making a study plan and practicing breathing techniques. Fear becomes focus.

Envy → Motivation
Scenario: A professional scrolling through social media sees a peer announcing a major career success. A pang of envy hits—tightness in the chest, self-comparison, resentment rising.
Old path: Rumination, bitterness, disengagement.
Redirection: Naming the feeling: *"This envy is showing*

me what I value but haven't pursued." Instead of stewing, the professional drafts a plan to build skills and reach out for mentorship. Envy becomes clarity of direction.

Sadness → Art
Scenario: After a painful breakup, someone feels a heavy sense of loss. Isolation, tears, and withdrawal dominate.
Old path: Numbing through alcohol, distraction, or despair.
Redirection: Treating sadness as signal energy: *"This is love's echo, a proof of deep connection."* They channel the feeling into songwriting and painting, producing works that speak to others in similar pain. Sadness becomes contribution.

Each of these cases illustrates the **Decode → Match → Channel** framework in motion. The instinct does not vanish—it is translated. Anger protects, fear focuses, envy clarifies, sadness connects. The same fuel that could destroy becomes the very energy that builds.

Exercises for Mastery:

Redirection, like any skill, strengthens through deliberate rehearsal. These exercises provide structured ways to practice turning raw impulse into intentional action until the process becomes second nature.

The "Before I React" Script
A simple, three-part pause designed to break automaticity in the moment:

- *Right now I feel ___. (Name the signal: anger, envy, fear, shame.)*

- *It's trying to ___. (Identify its evolutionary purpose: protect, compete, connect, retreat.)*

- *I choose to ___ instead. (Select a value-aligned redirection: set a boundary, plan, connect, create.)*

This script creates a gap between signal and action, giving space for authorship.

The Redirection Wheel Exercise

Visualize a wheel with impulses on the outer rim and constructive alternatives radiating inward. For example:

- **Anger** → assertive communication, problem-solving

- **Fear** → preparation, mindfulness grounding

- **Envy** → self-improvement plan, gratitude practice

- **Sadness** → creative expression, reaching out to community

- **Shame** → self-compassion, accountability conversation

By mapping multiple redirection options for each instinct, the wheel becomes a quick-reference guide. Over time, it conditions the brain to associate signals with constructive pathways.

Building a Personal Redirection Bank

Like an athlete rehearsing plays, individuals can pre-load responses before crisis moments.

- Identify 3–5 recurring triggers (e.g., jealousy in relationships, workplace frustration, fear before public speaking).
- For each, design 1–2 practiced redirection strategies.
- Rehearse mentally or physically so they become reflexes when the signal appears.

Example: *"When I feel stage fright, I redirect by breathing deeply, reframing it as energy for performance, and picturing a supportive face in the crowd."*

With repetition, the brain learns that instinctual energy has an outlet other than the default autopilot.

Together, these exercises transform redirection from a hopeful idea into a lived capability. They shift the nervous system's wiring—turning chaos into clarity, reaction into authorship.

Common Pitfalls:

Redirection is powerful, but like any skill, it can be misapplied. Not every "alternative action" is truly constructive. Some pathways only *mask* the signal instead of transforming it. These false redirects feel soothing in the moment but leave the underlying drive unresolved, often stronger when it resurfaces.

Substitution with Distractions

Scrolling endlessly on a phone, binge-watching, or compulsively checking notifications may quiet discomfort, but the signal is simply numbed—not redirected. The instinct's energy remains unintegrated.

Addictive Loops

Food, alcohol, gambling, or compulsive shopping can masquerade as coping mechanisms. They hijack the signal's energy but cycle it into dependency rather than authorship. Instead of channeling, the instinct is commodified.

Aggression in Disguise

Sometimes redirection takes the form of "productive hostility"—overworking, dominating conversations, or "winning" arguments under the banner of self-improvement. These are not redirections but rebrandings of the same raw impulse.

Over-Intellectualization

Thinking *about* the signal endlessly without ever moving into action is another false redirect. Reflection becomes avoidance, keeping energy trapped in analysis paralysis.

Denial Masquerading as Strength

Declaring "I'm fine" or "I don't care" may feel like control, but it is suppression in disguise. The energy goes underground, waiting for the next weak moment to burst through.

True Redirection has Three Markers:
- It *acknowledges* the signal openly.
- It *meets* the underlying evolutionary need in a value-aligned way.
- It *channels* the energy into momentum that strengthens agency.

Anything less risks perpetuating the autopilot.

Simply noticing signals is not enough; without redirection, impulses either fester underground as suppression or erupt outward as reaction.

Through scripts, exercises, and practiced strategies, redirection becomes not an act of willpower but a *trained reflex*. Over time, the nervous system rewires: jealousy can fuel growth, fear can sharpen planning, anger can strengthen boundaries, and shame can transform into accountability.

The key insight is this: impulse energy is not the enemy—it is raw material. When harnessed, it becomes momentum for authorship rather than captivity. With practice, redirection shifts from experiment to habit, from fragile effort to durable skill.

Chapter 10. Reflection and Design

The Power of Reflection:

Reflection is the human equivalent of debugging. Just as a programmer steps back from running code to examine where it succeeded and where it failed, reflection allows us to step out of the immediacy of our impulses and observe the **signal → response → outcome** chain with clarity. It is not about judgment, but about analysis: *What happened? Why did it happen? What can I learn for next time?*

This is where the practice of Autognosis deepens. Recognition shows us the signal. Separation creates space to observe, Redirection gives us a new path. But reflection allows us to see the loops—the repeating patterns of instinct and choice that define much of our behavior. By identifying these loops, we begin to map our personal operating system and expose its vulnerabilities.

It's important to distinguish **reflection** from **rumination**. Rumination circles endlessly around mistakes, fueling shame and paralysis. Reflection, in contrast, is constructive review. It is oriented toward adjustment, iteration, and growth. Rumination keeps the signal alive; reflection quiets it by extracting the lesson and encoding it for future use.

When practiced regularly, reflection turns daily life into a feedback-rich laboratory. A failed redirection attempt becomes data, not defeat. A repeated trigger becomes an invitation to design a protocol, not a condemnation of weakness. Over time, reflection creates a metacognitive layer—a part of the mind that watches, learns, and redesigns, ensuring that progress is not a random accident but a deliberate trajectory.

Reflection Tools:

Reflection becomes reliable when it is scaffolded with tools—structured methods that convert vague self-examination into clear, repeatable learning. The following practices help translate experience into insight:

Journaling Prompts

A daily or situational journal can transform fleeting impulses into recorded data. The simplest prompts are often the most powerful:

- *What signal repeated today?*
- *How did I respond?*
- *Did my response align with my values?*
- *What would I try differently next time?*

This practice shifts reflection from abstract musing into a record of patterns that can be revisited and tracked over time.

Behavior Audits

A behavior audit works like a flowchart, breaking experiences into their components:

- *Trigger → Signal → Response → Outcome → Adjustment*

By mapping the sequence, individuals see not only the signal but the linkages that carry it into action. Once these links are visible, they can be deliberately re-engineered.

Mirror Questions

Sometimes a single well-placed question can interrupt the tendency to rationalize or excuse a poor response. A useful mirror question is:

- *"What would the wiser version of me have done?"*
  This reframing lifts reflection out of the emotional residue of the moment and invites perspective-taking—consulting not guilt, but guidance.

Weekly Audits and Pattern Heat Maps

Over longer spans, reflection benefits from aggregation. Weekly reviews help reveal which signals dominate, where redirections succeed, and where autopilot still rules. Patterns can be visualized in a "heat map" of recurring signals—anger concentrated at work, shame tied to social media, fear arising in financial discussions. Seeing these hotspots allows individuals to target design interventions where they matter most.

Together, these tools turn reflection from an occasional afterthought into a systematic diagnostic discipline. They ensure that each experience, successful or not, becomes material for redesign.

The Transition to Design:

Reflection alone, while clarifying, is not sufficient. To pause and notice a repeating loop without acting upon it is like diagnosing a structural flaw but never reinforcing the building. Insight without architecture leaves the system vulnerable to collapse under stress.

This is where Design enters. If reflection is the act of seeing patterns, then design is the act of encoding corrections into structure. Reflection gives the blueprint; design lays the foundation.

Design transforms awareness into permanence. Instead of relying on willpower in each new situation, an individual pre-loads protocols, rituals, and values so that the system itself carries the weight of alignment. In this sense, design is less about control and more about automation: setting up reliable defaults that serve chosen ends rather than inherited impulses.

Without design, reflection risks turning into endless journaling or intellectual self-analysis—a treadmill of "knowing" without "becoming." With design, reflection becomes iterative: each audit informs an upgrade, each misstep seeds a more resilient framework.

The transition is therefore critical:

- **Reflection** identifies what is happening.
- **Design** ensures a different outcome the next time it does.

This pivot from *insight* to *architecture* marks the difference between people who chronically "know their patterns" but remain stuck in them, and those who deliberately build new defaults. Autognosis insists that only when design follows reflection does true authorship emerge.

Design Components:

If reflection is the diagnostic process, then design is the act of building durable systems. In Autognosis, design is not about rigid control but about encoding stability and intentionality into one's daily operating environment. The core components of this architecture are:

Values as the Foundation

Values form the ground upon which all else is built. They answer the question: *What is worth orienting toward?* Without values, every redirection becomes arbitrary—choices shift with mood or circumstance. With values, redirection becomes purposeful, tethered to something larger than the momentary impulse. Examples: integrity, compassion, growth, truth-seeking.

Principles as Rules of Engagement

Principles are values operationalized. They are if-then statements, guidelines for how to act when pressure tests arise. Where values are abstract, principles are applied.

- Value: *Honesty.*

- Principle: *"When tempted to hide the truth, I will pause and state it clearly, even if uncomfortable."*

Protocols as Pre-Loaded Scripts

Protocols are structured responses to recurring triggers. They remove the burden of improvisation in high-stress moments by giving the mind a well-worn path.

- Example: For anger, the protocol might be: *pause → breathe → state boundary in one sentence.*
- For fear before public speaking: *deep breath → anchor with first line → scan the room for supportive faces.*

These scripts preempt the hijack of impulse with intentional, rehearsed alternatives.

Rituals as Automated Stabilizers

Rituals keep the system aligned without requiring constant conscious effort. They serve as *background processes*—stabilizers that sustain momentum.

- Morning grounding rituals (stretch, breathe, set intention).
- Stress resets (walk, cold water splash, short mantra).
- End-of-week reviews (audit wins, identify adjustments).

Rituals automate virtue, making alignment habitual rather than exceptional.

Identity Stack as Modular, Upgradable Roles

Identity is not fixed—it is modular. The "identity stack" consists of the roles a person chooses to embody (parent, leader, student, creator). Each role can be upgraded like software—revised, expanded, or even retired. The stack allows flexibility without collapse: one can fail in a role without losing the self, because selfhood is distributed across modules.

Together, these five design components convert reflection into architecture. They ensure that lessons do not remain as fleeting insights but are embodied in daily living. With each iteration, the system grows sturdier, more aligned, and more capable of self-authorship.

Practical Exercises:

Reflection and design only take root when embodied in practice. The following exercises help translate abstract principles into concrete, lived systems.

Create a "Me Manual"

Think of this as a personal operations guide—a reference document for your own authorship.

- **Step 1: Define values.** List the 3–5 values that form your foundation (e.g., integrity, resilience, compassion, growth).

- **Step 2: Translate into principles.** For each value, write 1–2 principles that show how it applies in action.

- **Step 3: Include reset protocols.** Add routines you will use when destabilized (breathing techniques, grounding rituals, reflection cues).

The result is a living document that grows with you—a manual for who you are becoming, not just who you are.

Write and Rehearse Default Scripts

Signals strike fast, so the mind needs prepared responses. By scripting in advance, you preload intentional reactions.

- **Identify common triggers.** (e.g., anger in traffic, envy at work, shame in conflict).

- **Write scripts.** Example: "When I feel defensive, I will pause and say, 'Let me think about that before I respond.'"

- **Rehearse aloud.** Saying it in your own voice strengthens recall and reduces reaction time in live situations.

Over time, these scripts become the system's "if-then" code, stabilizing behavior under stress.

Construct a Personal Reflection Log and Feedback Loop

Without feedback, growth stalls. A reflection log keeps the system adaptive.

- **Daily check-in.** Write one or two notes: What signal showed up? How did I redirect? Was the outcome aligned?
- **Weekly audit.** Review your notes and highlight recurring patterns. Identify what worked and what needs redesign.
- **Heat mapping.** Over time, mark signals that appear most often. These become priority areas for refining protocols or designing new rituals.

The log becomes both mirror and compass: a record of where you have been, and a guide to where you are going.

Engineering Authorship:

What sets humans apart is not simply intelligence, but the ability to step outside of instinctual loops and re-engineer them. Animals can learn, adapt, and even display forms of culture, but they remain bound to the narrow circuitry of inherited drives. Humans alone possess the capacity for *systemic authorship*—to reflect on their patterns and deliberately design the structures that govern their lives.

- **Reflection** is the debug function. It lets us look back at the sequence—trigger → signal → response → outcome—and see where the system failed or succeeded. It is the meta-layer of awareness that allows course correction.
- **Design** is the upgrade function. It moves us beyond mere adaptation into intentional reconfiguration. By encoding values, principles,

and rituals, we create new default settings that persist across time.

Together, reflection and design elevate us from passengers of biology to pilots of selfhood. This is the *evolutionary leap*: moving from being shaped by the environment to shaping the systems that shape us.

Civilizations rise or fall based on whether they can make this leap collectively. A society without reflection calcifies into repetition. A society without design collapses into chaos. But when reflection identifies dysfunction and design encodes better systems, humanity transcends biology's constraints.

In Autognosis, this leap is not abstract—it is daily and personal. Every time an individual interrupts an old loop and installs a new protocol, they enact the same leap that once separated early humans from their primate ancestors. To reflect is to evolve in awareness. To design is to evolve in structure. Together, they constitute the defining human power: not just to survive, but to self-create.

Reflection and design are not optional add-ons but the very mechanisms by which freedom and authorship become durable. Reflection transforms instinct-driven episodes into lessons; design encodes those lessons into living systems. Together, they form the architecture of an intentional life.

Without reflection, we repeat; without design, we drift. But with both, we can consciously shape our daily actions and the trajectory of our identity.

Autognosis empowers each person to become the engineer of their own compass—one who can chart direction in alignment with chosen values, rather than being carried by inherited defaults. In this way, freedom ceases to be fragile and becomes structural, embedded in the routines and principles that guide action.

Part IV – The Horizon
Chapter 11. Autognosis in Society

Systems Mirror Biology:

Every society is, at its root, an amplification of biology. The same drives that surge through an individual nervous system—these obsolescent instincts—scale upward into the institutions we build. Nations posture like rival primates, corporations hoard like anxious gatherers, political factions harden into tribes. What begins as limbic reflex in the individual becomes codified as law, economy, and culture at scale.

Civilizations, therefore, are not abstract machines divorced from human nature. They are the living mirrors, constructed from the instincts of their participants. Where impulses go unexamined, systems inherit their distortions. Fear breeds surveillance states. Dominance consolidates into oligarchies. Tribal reflexes calcify into political polarization and sectarian strife. Scarcity anxiety fuels economic exploitation and environmental depletion.

What we call "systemic corruption" is often just biology in institutional form. The instinctual substrate of humanity, left unchecked, repeats itself in larger and more destructive loops. Just as an unreflective person confuses reaction for choice, unreflective societies confuse instinct for governance.

Autognosis challenges this fatalism. By teaching individuals to recognize, separate, and redirect their impulses, it inserts authorship where biology once reigned. And because systems are made of people, the practice of Autognosis at scale implies that institutions themselves can be redesigned—not through revolutions and upheaval, but through the steady accumulation of self-aware participants refusing to replicate primal defaults.

The lesson is stark but liberating: **civilizations don't fail because they are cursed, but because they are unconscious.** The same way an individual can transcend reaction, a culture can transcend its inherited reflexes. But the work begins inside the smallest unit—the human mind.

Education and Early Intervention:

If civilizations mirror biology, then their long-term stability depends on the biology they choose to cultivate. The earlier instinct literacy is taught, the less entrenched destructive defaults become. This is why education is not simply an accessory to Autognosis—it is its lifeline.

Children are born with reflexes honed by evolution: fear to ensure survival, belonging to secure protection, anger to defend against threats. These instincts are not flaws; they are inheritance. But without guidance, they calcify into lifelong habits of reaction. A child who learns only to obey impulse becomes an adult who mistakes tribal outrage for civic participation or consumption for fulfillment.

A curriculum that incorporates Autognosist principles could offers a direct response: a structured framework that introduces signal literacy from the start of life. In early childhood, this means simple naming of impulses ("I feel angry; my chest is tight"), stories that model redirection (a character who channels jealousy into collaboration), and rituals that create pauses before action. In adolescence, it becomes reflective journaling, role-playing ethical dilemmas, and mapping the five pillars of Autognosis—Recognition, Separation, Redirection, Reflection, Design—onto real-world challenges like peer pressure and digital addiction.

By embedding Autognosis into education, schools cease to be factories of rote information and instead become workshops of self-authorship. Each generation grows less likely to replicate the instinctual misfires of the one before.

Imagine a society where conflict resolution is taught as rigorously as mathematics, where ethical design is practiced alongside coding, where young adults graduate not only with career skills but with mastery of their own inner architecture.

The significance is this: generational ignorance perpetuates instinctual captivity; generational literacy builds a trajectory of conscious evolution. Just as literacy in reading reshaped civilizations by unlocking knowledge, signal literacy can reshape them again by unlocking agency.

Leadership and Governance:

Leadership, at its worst, is often little more than instinct scaled. History offers endless examples: rulers who mistake dominance for authority, parties that collapse into tribal conflict, institutions corrupted by fear of scarcity and loss. The result is predictable—cycles of power-hoarding, exploitation, and collapse. When leaders remain unconscious of the biology beneath their choices, governance becomes a theater of primal reflex dressed in the language of policy.

Autognosis offers an alternative: leadership as authorship, not instinctual reenactment. A leader trained in signal literacy can recognize when their own impulses are impacting their judgment. Instead of reacting, they separate from the impulse, examine it, and redirect it into ethical clarity. Decisions are then shaped not by what gratifies the limbic system in the moment, but by what aligns with long-term values and collective flourishing.

Consider a leader facing public criticism. The limbic reflex is defense: to attack, deny, or silence dissent. A self-aware leader, by contrast, can pause, identify the sting of status anxiety, and redirect it into transparency or dialogue. The outcome is not only healthier politics but healthier citizens, who see authority modeled as reflection rather than reaction.

At scale, Autognosis reshapes governance itself. Institutions led by individuals fluent in signal literacy can resist the gravitational pull of tribal polarization. Policies emerge less from the binary logic of "us vs.

them" and more from systemic design thinking: how to encode principles, rituals, and protocols that reduce corruption and foster trust.

In this sense, Autognostic leadership is not simply about making better choices; it is about building better systems. Leaders become architects of governance who understand that without intentional design, institutions merely replicate the worst of human biology. With it, they can author frameworks of justice, collaboration, and accountability that endure beyond any single administration.

Governance is, at root, applied biology. Autognosis turns it into applied authorship.

Justice and Conflict Resolution:

Crime and conflict are usually treated as moral failings or matters of "good versus evil." Yet from the lens of Autognosis, they are more often instinctual misfires that spill into destructive action.

- **Anger misfires** into violence.
- **Scarcity anxiety** drives theft or hoarding.
- **Dominance impulses** fuel coercion, exploitation, and abuse.
- **Tribal belonging** curdles into gang identity or sectarian conflict.

Traditional justice systems respond by suppressing the symptom: punishment, isolation, deterrence. But this often deepens the very signals it seeks to control—fear intensifies, shame corrodes, tribal bonds within prisons grow stronger. The cycle perpetuates itself, with "rehabilitation" reduced to containment.

An Autognosis-based approach reframes justice not as punishment but as signal literacy training. Instead of branding individuals as irredeemable, it equips them to recognize and redirect the instincts that led them astray:

- A violent offender learns to separate anger from aggression and channel it into constructive boundary-setting.

- A thief, driven by scarcity fear, is taught economic planning and resource-sharing rituals that stabilize the impulse.

- A gang member learns to disentangle the belonging signal from destructive tribal loyalty and redirect it into prosocial community-building.

Conflict resolution follows the same model. When disputes arise—between individuals, groups, or even nations—mediation is no longer about negotiation alone but about uncovering the underlying signals driving escalation. Fear, dominance, and shame can be surfaced, named, and redirected toward outcomes that preserve dignity and foster collaboration.

This shift does not erase accountability; it deepens it. By treating crime as a signal problem rather than a fixed identity, offenders are held responsible not merely for their actions but for their commitment to redesigning the systems within themselves. Justice becomes less about retribution and more about authorship—equipping individuals to write different scripts when the same impulses arise again.

If prisons taught Autognostic principles they would cease to be cages of containment and become academies of transformation. Such institutions would be less likely to produce hardened repeat offenders, instead graduates of self-authorship—individuals fluent in the same discipline society itself must practice if it is to escape its own cycles of collapse.

Justice, reframed through Autognosis, is not merely the end of harm; it is the beginning of design.

Economics and Resource Management:

At its root, economics is not simply about money—it is about how humans respond to the instinct of scarcity. For most of evolutionary history, resources were limited, unpredictable, and hard-won. Those who hoarded survived; those who shared too freely risked death. This wiring persists, but in the modern world it has been amplified and exploited.

- **Scarcity anxiety** becomes the engine of consumer capitalism, where endless acquisition is framed as security.
- **Hoarding impulses** metastasize into financial speculation, wealth concentration, and unsustainable extraction of natural resources.

- **Status anxiety**, piggybacking on scarcity, drives conspicuous consumption and the constant churn of desire.

The result is not security but fragility: debt cycles, ecological collapse, widening inequality. A species designed for famine management now undermines itself in an age of relative abundance.

Autognosis offers a different pathway: redirecting scarcity signals into stewardship.

- When fear of "not enough" arises, individuals and institutions can channel it into planning, resilience-building, and cooperative pooling rather than accumulation without end.

- Hoarding energy can be redirected into investment in regenerative systems—renewable energy, circular economies, shared infrastructure—that create long-term abundance rather than short-term gain.

- Status anxiety can be reframed: instead of competing through consumption, cultures can elevate contribution, wisdom, and sustainability as new markers of esteem.

Some glimpses of this already exist: community co-ops that replace competitive markets, degrowth movements that emphasize sufficiency over excess, and regenerative business models that measure success in ecological health rather than quarterly profit. These are not just moral stances—they are signal redesigns. They teach humans to feel the pull of scarcity and respond with creativity, not exploitation.

At scale, such redirection would alter the very DNA of economies. Capitalism's engine of endless growth, built on hijacked instincts, could be replaced with an economy of enough: one that honors human drives while steering them toward sustainability. Scarcity would no longer be a lever for manipulation, but a prompt for collaboration.

The lesson is clear: without Autognosis, economic systems will continue to mirror primitive hoarding behaviors, dragging both civilization and the biosphere toward collapse. With it, instinct becomes not a curse but a resource—fuel for building economies designed to endure.

In mastering scarcity within ourselves, we master sustainability in the world.

Media and Culture:

If economics is where scarcity instincts are monetized, media is where tribalism and outrage are weaponized.

Digital platforms thrive on attention, and attention is most easily captured by triggering primal signals. Fear sharpens focus. Outrage rallies tribes. Shame enforces conformity. Algorithms are not neutral —they are instinct amplifiers.

- **Outrage cycles**: A single post can ignite anger, which spreads faster than reasoned dialogue because the brain is wired to prioritize threats.

- **Tribal echo chambers**: Platforms sort people into identity groups where belonging is reinforced and outsiders are demonized.
- **Shame spirals**: Public call-outs trigger the instinct to conform or retaliate, rather than to reflect or reform.

The result is a cultural environment where instincts—not authorship—set the tone. The more divided, reactive, and compulsive users become, the more profitable the system is for those who design it.

Autognosis offers a counter-literacy: signal awareness as resistance.

- When a post makes the pulse quicken, the practiced mind asks: *Is this fear or anger being triggered?*
- When tribal instincts flare—*They're against us*—the literate person can pause and see the biology beneath the rhetoric.
- When shame appears online, the trained response is not automatic retreat or counterattack, but conscious evaluation: *Is this signal aligned with my values, or is it being manipulated?*

At the individual level, this creates resilience. Outrage bait loses its grip. Polarizing narratives are recognized as primitive triggers rather than ultimate truths. Online interactions shift from unconscious reaction to conscious authorship.

At the cultural level, the implications are transformative. A society fluent in signals cannot be as easily divided or manipulated. Platforms designed around outrage would lose their dominance, replaced—eventually—by ones that reward depth, nuance, and collaborative problem-solving.

Autognosis does not call for withdrawal from digital life, but for a new kind of participation. The same way literacy once transformed oral societies—making individuals less vulnerable to rumor and more capable of reflection—signal literacy could transform digital societies, making individuals less captive to outrage and more capable of dialogue.

In learning to read our own biology online, we reclaim authorship of culture itself.

Institutional Case Studies:

To understand the societal stakes of Autognosis, it helps to imagine how history might have unfolded differently if signal literacy had been embedded in leadership, institutions, or the public at large. These examples are not fantasies of perfection, but illustrations of how instinct recognition and redirection could have changed trajectories.

The Cuban Missile Crisis (1962)

- **Instinct at play:** Fear (nuclear annihilation) + dominance (refusal to appear weak).
- **Historical risk:** A hair-trigger instinct for retaliation could have escalated into global war.

- **Counterfactual with Autognosis:** Leaders trained to read their own signals might have recognized fear's grip on their judgments and dominance's demand for posturing. Reflection and redirection could have encouraged earlier backchannel negotiation and less brinkmanship, lowering the risk of catastrophic miscalculation.

The Rwandan Genocide (1994)

- **Instinct at play:** Tribal belonging + fear + dominance.

- **Historical risk:** Dehumanization spirals triggered mass violence.

- **Counterfactual with Autognosis:** A population trained in signal literacy would be better able to identify how tribal instincts were being manipulated by propaganda. Recognizing the biology behind fear and dominance could have enabled resistance to manipulative calls for extermination, fostering pockets of refusal and slowing the spread of violence.

The 2008 Global Financial Crisis

- **Instinct at play:** Hoarding + status anxiety + short-term reward.

- **Historical risk:** Financial institutions amplified scarcity and greed instincts, leading to systemic collapse.

- **Counterfactual with Autognosis:** Signal-aware leaders and regulators could have recognized hoarding behavior disguised as innovation. Reflection on the evolutionary pull of short-term gain could have motivated redirection toward principles of sustainability, transparency, and systemic resilience.

Climate Change (Ongoing)

- **Instinct at play:** Scarcity avoidance (consume before others), repetition bias ("keep things the same"), and denial (shielding from fear).

- **Historical risk:** Collective inertia and overconsumption drive ecological collapse.

- **Counterfactual with Autognosis:** A citizenry fluent in signals would see consumption urges as biological—not warrant—and redirect them toward sufficiency and stewardship. Leaders trained in Autognosis could resist the dominance logic of industrial competition, instead designing cooperative protocols for planetary survival.

Hypothetical Future – AI Governance

- **Instinct at play:** Dominance (race to control), fear (job loss, extinction), tribalism (national competition).

- **Risk:** Nations could allow biological impulses to dictate reckless AI escalation.

- **With Autognosis:** Leaders fluent in instinct literacy would separate legitimate caution from fear spirals, redirect dominance away from competition toward collaboration, and design principles to align technological growth with ethical clarity.

These cases show that **institutions mirror the instincts of those who run them.** Without literacy, those instincts play out unexamined—fueling wars, crises, and collapses. With Autognosis, leaders and citizens alike could redirect those same impulses toward survival, cooperation, and progress.

Objections and Challenges:

Any proposal to extend a personal philosophy into the architecture of society will invite resistance. Skeptics will ask: *Can something as intimate as signal literacy truly scale into governance, economics, or culture?* This concern is not trivial—many philosophies falter when stretched from the individual to the collective. Autognosis must meet this challenge directly.

"Human nature is fixed; people don't change."
This objection assumes that instincts are immutable. Yet neuroscience demonstrates plasticity: brains rewire with practice, habits form through repetition, and cultures shift over generations. Just as literacy in reading or mathematics was once rare but is now foundational, signal literacy can be cultivated until it becomes normal.

"Personal practice cannot alter institutions."
History shows otherwise. Movements that reshaped societies—abolition, civil rights, democracy itself—began with individual redefinitions of self and spread

through networks of practice. When enough individuals adopt a new lens, institutions follow. Culture is downstream from consciousness.

"This is idealistic; real power runs on dominance and fear."
True: many systems are presently driven by dominance instincts. But this is precisely the point. Autognosis does not deny biology—it names it, exposes it, and offers redirection. Power built on fear is brittle; power built on authorship and alignment is resilient. The question is not whether dominance exists, but whether it remains the only language we allow to structure our societies.

"It risks misuse—who decides what values should guide redirection?"
This is a crucial challenge. Autognosis cannot impose values without becoming authoritarian. Instead, it teaches a meta-skill: recognizing impulses and choosing in alignment with *one's declared values*. The discipline lies not in dictating what to believe, but in ensuring that beliefs are consciously authored rather than inherited or manipulated. The responsibility for ethical design remains personal, though it flourishes within communities of accountability.

"Scaling takes too long; crises are urgent."

Indeed, cultural rewiring is slow. But so was literacy, public health, and education reform—and each transformed the world. Autognosis is not an overnight solution; it is an intergenerational discipline. Its urgency lies not in instant results but in planting the seeds of change now, so that future societies inherit tools beyond instinctual autopilot.

In summary:

Autognosis does not claim to erase instinct or deliver utopia. It claims only this: that without literacy, we remain captives of biology, with it, we gain authorship. Change begins at the smallest scale—one person practicing recognition, separation, redirection—and scales outward, accumulating into cultural momentum. Institutions will shift when the minds inside them shift first.

Every institution—schools, governments, markets, media—mirrors the instincts of the individuals who compose it. When those instincts remain unexamined, they scale into corruption, exploitation, tribalism, and collapse. Therefore, Autognosis is not only a path of personal development but a civic necessity.

But when individuals cultivate signal literacy, practice redirection, and embed reflection into design, they generate new defaults: leadership that resists dominance, economies that temper scarcity with sustainability, media that values clarity over outrage, and cultures that expand belonging without conformity.

Culture is not imposed from above but authored through countless micro-decisions at the level of the individual nervous system. To practice Autognosis privately is therefore to contribute to public evolution. To neglect it is to allow ancient impulses to continue scripting the future unchecked.

Autognosis offers a bridge between the self and society. It reminds us that freedom is not an inheritance but a discipline, and that civilizations rise or fall according to whether their members remain captives of biology or authors of design.

Chapter 12. Autognosis and the Future

The Next Evolutionary Leap:

For most of history, human evolution was written in flesh. Natural selection worked slowly, sculpting traits over millennia—sharper eyes, stronger muscles, more efficient metabolisms. But that age is over. The survival challenges we now face are not biological predators or physical scarcity; they are products of our own minds and machines. Nuclear arsenals, algorithmic manipulation, ecological collapse—these are crises born not of genetic weakness but of instinctual misfires scaled by technology.

In this new epoch, evolution is no longer primarily genetic. It's cognitive and behavioral. Humanity's next leap will not be a taller frame or stronger lungs but a more skillful nervous system—one that can step outside its own limbic defaults. The species that once survived by fighting, hoarding, and dividing must now learn to survive by redirecting those very drives.

Autognosis offers the blueprint for this leap. If we think of civilization as an operating system, our current version is still running on legacy code: territorial reflexes, tribal loyalty, dominance hierarchies. These routines were efficient in the savannah, but catastrophic when amplified by nuclear weapons, climate destabilization, and AI-powered propaganda. Without a deliberate upgrade, humanity risks running fatal errors in its own system.

The upgrade is not genetic engineering, or cybernetic augmentation—it is behavioral authorship. Autognosis reframes instinct from unalterable command to malleable input, allowing individuals—and by extension, cultures—to choose their outputs. It is the software patch humanity must install to survive its own inventions.

Just as literacy once transformed civilization by freeing thought from the prison of oral memory, signal literacy and redirection can free humanity from the prison of limbic reactivity. This is not a luxury or a niche practice—it is the condition for survival in the centuries ahead.

The next evolutionary leap is not biological or technological. It's the deliberate authorship of behavior itself.

Technology and AI:

If instincts are the raw code of biology, then modern technology has become the amplifier—an exponential echo chamber that magnifies every limbic signal. Social media algorithms prioritize outrage because fear and anger hold attention. Recommendation systems reward tribal conformity because belonging drives clicks. Notifications exploit novelty-seeking instincts by delivering unpredictable micro-rewards, pulling users into compulsive loops.

The result is a civilization in which our oldest impulses are continuously provoked by our newest inventions. Instead of tools serving human authorship, the tools exploit human autopilot. This is not malicious intent alone—it is structural. Attention markets monetize reactivity, so the systems evolve to favor what keeps users locked in cycles of fear, division, and craving.

Here Autognosis provides a dual framework: user resistance and designer responsibility.

- **For users**, signal literacy becomes digital armor. Recognizing the bodily jolt of outrage, the shallow breath of status anxiety, or the dopamine tug of novelty craving allows a pause before the click. The practiced skill of redirection—stepping back, reframing, choosing a different engagement—reclaims authorship from the algorithm's bait. The person ceases to be a product and becomes again a participant.

- **For designers**, Autognosis introduces an ethical frontier. If algorithms are extensions of human cognition, they must not merely reinforce limbic defaults but embed reflective logic. This means platforms designed to reward long-term value over short-term reaction: promoting deliberation, encouraging diverse dialogue rather than tribal silos, offering prompts for reflection instead of feeding endless reflex. In effect, Autognosis becomes a design philosophy for humane technology.

The critical point is this: **AI and algorithms are not inherently corrosive—they mirror the instincts we feed them.** Without conscious authorship, they calcify our reactivity into systems of manipulation. With Autognosis as a guide, they could instead become scaffolds for awareness, nudging individuals and societies toward reflection, balance, and ethical clarity.

The challenge of the AI age is not intelligence but alignment. Without instinct literacy, technology aligns with our worst impulses. With it, we have the chance to align machines with our highest authorship.

Post-Instinctual Civilization:

What would a world look like if its systems were no longer engineered by instinctual reflexes—fear, dominance, tribalism, hoarding—but by individuals practicing conscious authorship? The shift is not utopian fantasy; it is the logical extension of Autognosis applied at scale.

Governance Beyond Dominance and Tribalism

- Current political structures are built on competitive tribal signaling—parties, factions, dominance displays, zero-sum contests for power.

- A post-instinctual model emphasizes **cooperative governance**, where deliberation is rewarded over provocation, and consensus-building is seen as strength rather than weakness.

- Leaders trained in signal literacy recognize when their fear or dominance drives decision-making, and redirect toward ethical clarity. Conflict becomes something to metabolize, not exploit.

Sustainable Economies Beyond Hoarding and Scarcity

- Consumer capitalism thrives on instinctual scarcity and status anxiety—accumulate, consume, display.

- In a post-instinctual economy, **value creation aligns with sufficiency and stewardship.** Growth is measured not by extraction but by durability, regeneration, and equitable distribution.

- Hoarding instincts are redirected into systems of shared security—cooperative ownership models, resource cycles designed to endure generations, economies of enough rather than economies of more.

Ethical AI Alignment Beyond Reflex Amplification

- Today's machine intelligence mirrors our unexamined instincts: outrage drives feeds, novelty drives addiction, dominance drives competition.

- A post-instinctual design philosophy builds **AI systems that prioritize reflection over reflex.** Algorithms nudge toward diverse dialogue, ethical trade-offs, and long-term sustainability rather than short-term gratification.

- Autognosis provides the blueprint: if users learn to redirect impulses, designers can build technologies that assist in that redirection rather than exploit the lack of it.

The essence of a post-instinctual civilization is this: **systems cease to be extensions of animal reflexes and become extensions of conscious authorship.** Where fear once made armies, dominance made empires, and scarcity made exploitation, reflection and design now create institutions resilient to our primal defaults.

Such a civilization would not be free of conflict or desire—but its participants would possess the literacy to recognize instinct at the root of those tensions, and the design tools to redirect them toward constructive outcomes.

Post-instinctual civilization is not a distant dream—it is the next rational step in human evolution once Autognosis becomes widely practiced.

Environmental Imperatives:

Civilization's greatest challenge—ecological collapse—is not a mystery of technology, but of psychology. The engines of environmental destruction run on instincts that evolved for survival in scarcity but now backfire in abundance.

The Instinctual Roots of Collapse

- **Hoarding reflex**: Once vital for winter survival, it now manifests as unchecked accumulation—consuming resources far beyond need.

- **Short-term bias**: The brain prioritizes immediate gratification over long-range consequences, a trait that helped ancestors survive but sabotages climate policy, conservation, and intergenerational planning.

- **Territorial dominance**: Nations cling to resources as symbols of power, prioritizing competitive extraction over cooperative preservation.

From Instinct to Collapse

- These reflexes translate directly into modern ecological crises: deforestation for immediate profit, fossil fuel addiction despite known consequences, oceans treated as dumps because long-term effects feel abstract.

- Climate change is not only a technological failure—it is a failure of instinct literacy. Unexamined impulses scale into planetary breakdown.

Autognosis as Stewardship

- Signal literacy teaches individuals to **notice the scarcity reflex** ("I need to stockpile, consume, protect now") and redirect it toward collective sufficiency.

- Reflection cultivates the ability to stretch time horizons: **choosing long-term thriving over short-term reward.**

- Design encodes sustainability into daily practice—rituals of conservation, principles of restraint, protocols for resource sharing.

A Post-Instinctual Ecology

- Imagine economies designed not on hoarding but on **circular use**: every product recycled, every waste stream repurposed.

- Imagine governance not trapped in election cycles but oriented toward **seventh-generation stewardship**—a horizon beyond any individual lifespan.

- Imagine individuals who no longer feel scarcity as panic, but as a cue to innovate, cooperate, and sustain.

The environmental crisis reveals a stark truth: **ecology is a mirror of psychology.** The same instincts that once ensured survival now endanger it. Only by overriding those instincts—through Autognosis—can humanity adopt a stance of stewardship that matches the scale of the planet's needs.

In this sense, environmental repair is not merely technical but existential: it demands the evolution of human behavior itself.

The Risk of Regression:

Every step forward in human civilization has carried the shadow of regression—the pull of ancient instincts reasserting themselves under new conditions. The danger now is not stagnation, but collapse, as technologies amplify impulses faster than wisdom can restrain them.

Tribal Wars Amplified by Technology

- The tribal reflex, once limited to villages and clans, now operates at global scale.

- Digital platforms weaponize belonging and outrage, transforming political disagreements into existential conflicts.

- With nuclear arsenals and cyberweapons at hand, what was once a campfire quarrel can escalate into systemic collapse.

Dominance Hierarchies Encoded into AI

- Left unchecked, artificial intelligence will not be neutral. It will reflect the impulses of its creators.

- Algorithms optimized for profit already reinforce dominance—rewarding the loudest, most aggressive, most divisive voices.

- Without Autognosis guiding design, AI risks becoming an **amplifier of limbic reflexes**, locking hierarchy, greed, and tribalism into code.

Resource Exhaustion from Unchecked Hoarding

- The hoarding instinct, harmless when limited to grain silos, becomes catastrophic when scaled to planetary extraction.

- Water tables collapse, forests vanish, oceans acidify—not because humanity lacks alternatives, but because instinct screams louder than foresight.

- In this trajectory, collapse is not sudden—it is incremental, a death by accumulation.

The Regression Spiral

- As scarcity worsens, instincts intensify: fear breeds conflict, conflict fuels dominance, dominance accelerates hoarding, hoarding deepens scarcity.

- This spiral risks locking humanity into a **feedback loop of regression**—a civilization technologically advanced but psychologically primitive, consuming itself from within.

Autognosis is presented here not as luxury philosophy but as **a break-glass necessity.** Without conscious authorship, every technological gain becomes a sharper tool for instinctual misfires. The danger is not that humanity will fail to progress—but that it will progress into its own undoing.

The question is not whether humanity can build more powerful tools. It is whether humanity can evolve the **behavioral maturity** to wield them without collapse.

Speculative Horizons:

Autognosis, though rooted in the immediate work of individual practice, holds horizons far beyond the self. If signal literacy and redirection become as natural as reading and writing, the ripple effects extend across centuries and even into futures not yet imaginable.

Global Autognosis Education

Imagine a world where children grow up learning to identify jealousy alongside the alphabet, or to name shame as readily as they name colors. A global rollout of Autognosis-informed curricula could normalize instinctual literacy as a baseline human skill. Over generations, cycles of tribalism, fear, and dominance would lose their grip, replaced by a population fluent in authorship.

Leadership as Conscious Design

In such a future, leadership training would begin not with rhetoric or economics, but with the internal architecture of the self. Leaders would be evaluated not merely on charisma or policy positions but on their demonstrated ability to redirect impulses, to resist the intoxicating pull of dominance, and to govern with reflective clarity. A cabinet of Autognosis-trained leaders could become a stabilizing counterforce to the chaos of instinct-driven governance.

Preparing for Post-Earth Civilizations

As humanity extends outward—colonies on Mars, orbital stations, interstellar travel—the dangers of unrefined instinct will multiply. Small, high-stress communities cannot survive if tribalism, dominance, and scarcity reflexes dictate behavior. In this context, Autognosis becomes more than philosophy—it is survival training for post-Earth civilizations. A species unable to govern its instincts will not govern its colonies; it will fracture, consume, or implode.

The Long Arc of Speculation

From the classroom to the cosmos, Autognosis points to the possibility of a civilization authored rather than inherited. The speculative horizon is not utopia, but resilience: a human story that no longer ends in self-destruction, but in the conscious crafting of futures worthy of survival.

Ethics of the Future:

Traditional moral systems rely on static commandments or cultural norms. These are brittle in the face of novelty. Genetic engineering, artificial intelligence, post-Earth colonization—each presents scenarios unimagined by ancient traditions. What was once adaptive may now be destructive; what was once taboo may become survival. Autognosis sidesteps dogma by grounding ethics in self-authorship, a process adaptable to any terrain.

The Autognostic Ethical Lens

At its core, the lens asks:

- *What instinct is driving this impulse?*

- *Does acting on it align with conscious values or inherited defaults?*
- *What design choice creates resilience for both the individual and the collective?*

This process does not prescribe outcomes—it trains the capacity to generate them responsibly.

Moral Flexibility Without Relativism

Autognosis does not dissolve morality into "anything goes." Instead, it anchors ethics in transparency of impulse and fidelity to chosen values. It creates a flexible yet stable foundation: one where individuals and societies can face unknown conditions without regressing into instinctual chaos.

The Survival of Wisdom

In this framing, survival in the future is not guaranteed by stronger weapons, faster algorithms, or more efficient markets. It is guaranteed by wisdom—the ability to notice when the limbic system is steering civilization toward collapse, and to redirect before disaster. Autognosis is the mechanism by which that wisdom becomes a collective skill rather than an individual accident.

Human evolution has shifted from biology to behavior: the decisive question is whether we can master our instincts before our technologies amplify them beyond control.

Autognosis equips individuals with the literacy to resist manipulation, the discipline to design new patterns, and the ethical framework to face futures without precedent. Its promise is not utopia, but resilience—the ability to meet the unknown without collapsing into primitive reflexes.

The future will not be decided by the strength of our tools, but by the **maturity of our responses**. Autognosis offers the blueprint for that maturity: a skill of conscious authorship, scalable from individual to civilization, and indispensable for humanity's next leap.

Chapter 13. Invitation to the Reader

The Threshold Question:

Every philosophy, every movement, every transformation begins at a single point: a threshold. You now stand at yours.

The question is not abstract. It is immediate, visceral, and deeply personal:

Am I living by design—or by default?

Default means drifting with the current of inherited biology—acting on the signals that whisper, shout, or surge through your nervous system without question. It means waking, working, consuming, competing, fearing, and reacting in patterns older than civilization itself. Default is easy. It asks nothing but surrender.

Design is harder. Design requires awareness, pause, and authorship. It demands that you separate the signal from the self, recognize the ancient code at work, and then choose—not once, but again and again—how that energy will be expressed. Design is not about perfection; it is about direction. It is the conscious act of steering rather than drifting.

This threshold is not ceremonial. It is not waiting in some distant future after more reading, study, or preparation. It is here, in this moment, as your eyes move across this page.

The choice is yours: continue by default, or begin by design.

That is the threshold question. And it can only be answered in the living of your next breath, your next decision, your next act of authorship.

The Mirror Moment:

Before you step forward, pause here. Hold a mirror up to what has unfolded across these pages.

You have seen the **autopilot condition**—the truth that much of human life runs not on conscious intention but on reflexes encoded long before history began. The tribal pull, the fear reflex, the drive to dominate, the scramble to hoard—these are not your failures, but your inheritance.

You have glimpsed the **hidden code**—biology's quiet algorithms firing beneath awareness, shaping thought, emotion, and behavior. What felt personal has roots in the species itself. Autognosis unmasks this code, not to condemn it, but to give you the option of authorship.

You have encountered the **possibility of authorship**—the radical claim that you can learn to see the signal, step outside of it, and choose your response. That the energy of instinct need not dictate fate, but can be redirected into alignment with your chosen values.

You have walked through the **five pillars**:

- **Signal Literacy** — learning to recognize and name the impulses that move you.

- **Separation** — creating space between signal and self.
- **Redirection** — transforming raw energy into constructive action.
- **Reflection** — auditing your patterns, learning from loops.
- **Design** — encoding intentional systems into your life.

And you have stood before the **promise of a post-instinctual civilization**—a vision of humanity that transcends the cycles of fear and dominance, building systems authored by conscious design rather than inherited reflex.

This is your mirror moment. What you see is not a philosophy "out there" but a reflection of yourself—your biology, your potential, and the choice now placed in your hands.

Personal Agency:

No one can do this work for you.

Not an institution, not a government, not even the most devoted teacher or guide. Autognosis cannot be outsourced. It is **sovereign, individual, and daily.**

A school can introduce you to the vocabulary. A mentor can walk beside you as you practice. A community can encourage and remind you. But the moment of override—the pause between signal and response—belongs only to you.

It happens in the silence of your own nervous system:

- When fear rises, only you decide whether it becomes retreat or preparation.
- When anger flashes, only you choose whether it becomes destruction or assertion.
- When envy stirs, only you direct whether it becomes resentment or inspiration.

This is why Autognosis cannot be reduced to dogma, doctrine, or external enforcement. Any attempt to legislate it would hollow it out. The essence of Autognosis is freedom—authorship of your own behavior in the face of inherited reflex.

Every morning, you step into a new practice. Every signal that surfaces is another chance. The work is not grandiose; it is **ordinary and continuous**. It is how you speak to a colleague under stress, how you respond to your partner's need, how you meet your own insecurities with clarity instead of disguise.

Your life is the training ground. And only you can walk it.

The Scale of Impact:

Autognosis begins in the private interior, but its consequences never stay private.

Every choice you make—every signal you override, every impulse you redirect—shifts not only your life but the systems you inhabit.

- When a parent breaks a cycle of reactive anger, they rewrite the emotional inheritance of a household.

- When a leader pauses before responding with dominance, they reshape the climate of an organization.

- When a citizen resists the lure of outrage and chooses clarity, they tilt the balance of public discourse.

Culture is nothing more than the sum of individual reflexes, scaled and amplified. Which means culture can also be reshaped by individual authorship, scaled and amplified.

Your practice is not just personal—it is **civic.** Every time you choose authorship over autopilot, you weaken the grip of tribalism, fear, and exploitation on the systems around you. You become a subtle but undeniable force of correction.

This is why the practice matters. Because you do not stand apart from the world; you are the world in miniature. The way you live your signals is the way society lives its institutions.

To take responsibility for yourself is to take responsibility for the whole.

The Invitation:

The question is not when to begin. It is whether you will begin.

Autognosis is not a philosophy to admire from a distance. It is a practice to live, here and now, in the immediacy of your next action.

You do not need a course, a teacher, or a lifetime of study to start. You need only one moment of noticing.

- Notice one signal. A flicker of envy, a stab of fear, the tightness of anger in your chest.
- Separate from it. Remember: this is data, not truth.
- Redirect it. Choose the channel that aligns with your values instead of your reflex.
- Reflect and design differently. Record the loop, learn from it, and strengthen your authorship for tomorrow.

That's all. One step. One signal. One act of authorship.

Begin today. Begin now.

Because every moment you delay is another moment ceded to default. And every moment you choose authorship, you rewire not just yourself but the future of the culture you belong to.

Autognosis is not waiting in theory. It is waiting in practice—waiting in you.

Closing Vision:

Imagine yourself standing before a threshold. Behind you lies the familiar path of instinct, well-worn by generations before you—safe, automatic, predictable. Before you lies a bridge, not built yet, but waiting to be shaped by your steps. Each plank is laid as you walk, each direction chosen as you decide.

In your hand, a compass glows. Its needle does not point north but inward—to values, to authorship, to the life you are capable of designing.

A flame burns beside you—not the fire of anger or fear, but the steady light of awareness. It does not consume. It illuminates. It shows the hidden code, the impulses beneath the surface, and the power you have to redirect them.

The invitation is simple: step forward. Carry the flame, follow the compass, cross the threshold. The bridge appears only when you choose to walk it.

Autognosis is not a promise of perfection, but of authorship. It is the assurance that you are not bound to repeat the loops of the past. You are free to write, to design, to create a self and a society that reflect chosen values rather than inherited reflexes.

The page now turns to you. The flame is yours. The compass is in your hand. The threshold is waiting.

Step into authorship.

By the close of this chapter—and this book—you stand at the threshold of choice. Autognosis is no longer a set of ideas on a page, but a living practice that waits for your authorship. The core insight is simple yet radical: you are not bound to default instinct, nor condemned to repeat the patterns of your ancestors. You can pause, redirect, and design differently.

The path of Autognosis is not a theory to admire but a discipline to embody. Each moment you notice a signal and choose authorship over autopilot, you contribute not only to your own life but to the cultural fabric that surrounds you. One choice scales into many, one reflection into a new pattern, one author into a new future.

You are invited to begin now —not tomorrow, not in abstraction, but in the very next impulse you feel. Carry the flame of awareness, hold the compass of values, step across the threshold, and walk the bridge of your own design.

Afterword

Autognosis is not a destination but a discipline. These pages cannot replace the work of practice—nor should they. They can only point to the path, trace its contours, and offer tools for those willing to walk it. What matters begins after this final page: when signals rise, impulses press, and you decide whether to fall into old grooves or to author a new response.

The invitation is simple yet pivotal: begin small, begin today. Notice one signal. Pause. Name it. Redirect it. Reflect on the outcome. With repetition, these small acts accumulate into a new architecture of selfhood—an inner system built by intention rather than accident.

Autognosis belongs to no one, and yet to everyone. It is a commons of consciousness, a literacy to be practiced in solitude and shared in community. Its strength does not come from institutions or declarations, but in the daily authorship of individuals choosing to evolve beyond instinct.

If even a fraction take up this practice in earnest, humanity's trajectory bends. That is the wager of this philosophy, and the hope of this book.

I hope that you carry this new compass into the moments ahead. May it orient you toward authorship, design, freedom, and the world we have yet to build.

www.ingramcontent.com/pod-product-compliance
Lightning Source LLC
Chambersburg PA
CBHW070627030426
42337CB00020B/3936